DOWN TO EARTH

Land Demand in the New South Africa

Tessa Marcus, Kathy Eales
and Adèle Wildschut

Land and Agriculture Policy Centre

March 1996
Indicator Press
University of Natal

Editor: Karen Mac Gregor
Production and Design: Rob Evans
Production Assistant: Marion Evans
Proofreading: Peta Lee, Sarah Frost
and Dorothy Andrews
Cover painting: Louisa Wassenaar
Reproduction: Multigraphics
Printing: Creda Press

Indicator Press
CSDS, University of Natal
Private Bag X10, Dalbridge 4014
Durban, South Africa

Land and Agriculture Policy Centre
P O Box 243
WITS 2050
Johannesburg, South Africa

ISBN: 1-86840-182-0

FOREWORD

Derek Hanekom, Minister of Land Affairs

Land policy, especially land reform, has been shaped by the remarkable struggle of black people against forced dispossession under apartheid. By documenting the demands and needs of the landless, the Land Reform Research Programme has played an important role in contributing to the formulation of land policy.

Down to Earth gives us a glimpse of the hopes and aspirations of our landless people, and tells us about how lives might be transformed through land reform. Today's expressed aspirations are based on the opportunities people received at the time of the research, and we should not regard these as fixed or unchanging.

Research will always have an important role in informing policy. Policy makers need to know about people's realities on the ground – what they do, how they do it, and why. What do people need to bring about a real improvement in their lives? Do the laws need to be changed? Are new institutions necessary? The answers to these questions only come through thorough participatory research. We look forward to benefiting from the ongoing efforts of the research programme.

A word of thanks to the many researchers who participated in this project, to the countless community members who provided the information and to Danida, which had the foresight to become involved in land reform before it was government policy.

PREFACE

David Cooper, Director, Land and Agriculture Policy Centre

South Africa's first democratic Government has made land reform one of its top priorities and a cornerstone of its plans for reconstruction and development. It is hoped that land redistribution – along with restitution and tenure reform – will return land to black South Africans dispossessed of their land over centuries, and contribute to the upliftment of people who were systematically oppressed by apartheid.

The Land Reform Research Programme began in 1994, before the formation of the Government of National Unity and at a time when there was considerable uncertainty about whether there would be land reform in South Africa.

In mid-1993, the Land Reform Options Conference had set out some general ideas about how a land reform programme could be formulated, but there was concern that the ideas were not based on significant research among the communities which might be participants in a land reform programme.

The Land and Agriculture Policy Centre (LAPC) research was undertaken to ensure that the voices of poor rural people were heard before major policy decisions were made.

Their summary in *Down to Earth* is intended to provide readers with an insight into the experience of rural life as well as the hopes and aspirations of millions of South Africans.

The Land Reform Research Programme was the first comprehensive study ever conducted into land demand among black South Africans dispossessed under apartheid. It collected data from more than 60 sites in all nine provinces, and involved more than 100 researchers.

The research is part of ongoing work to develop a comprehensive land reform programme. It seeks to inform policy, not to provide policy, and is thus complementary to the important work being undertaken by the Department of Land Affairs. The intention is that the work begun in 1994 will be continued into a second phase of research in 1996/1997.

The LAPC would like to thank the authors of *Down to Earth*, the researchers who dedicated long hours to compiling data which was difficult to access and to finalising their reports, the communities who provided information, and Danida which funded the project generously.

ACKNOWLEDGEMENTS

There are literally thousands of people to thank for *Down to Earth*, since thousands of people offered the information on which it is based. However, there are several people whose input and advice were crucial to the book, and they should be mentioned by name.

Karen Mac Gregor, Editor, Indicator Press

The authors – Tessa Marcus, Kathy Eales and Adèle Wildschut – spent weeks ploughing through scores of bulky reports produced by the more than 100 researchers involved in the LAPC's Land Reform Research Programme, before they could even begin to write the book. Tessa Marcus in particular took on the responsibility of conceptualising themes from the huge amount of material.

I suspect that David Cooper, director of the LAPC, got a few grey hairs as he watched, guided and worried about the process. Thanks to him, and to Theresa Plewman and Elaine Cosser of the LAPC, for their efforts.

David Cooper should also be thanked, along with Saliem Fakir, for making a large contribution to the chapter on resource management, and Peter Rutsch for writing the chapter on tenure and land reform.

The task of writing *Down to Earth* was made easier by the efforts of the Programme's regional coordinators, who managed the research in the nine provinces and pulled it together into summary reports.

They were Pali Lehohla (North West), Dave Husy (Mpumalanga), Kgotoki Nhlapo (Gauteng), Dave Perkins (Northern Cape), Wim van Averbeke (Eastern Cape), Ntshine Moroka (Free State), Simon Foster (Northern Province), Harold Wesso (Western Cape) and Tessa Marcus (KwaZulu-Natal).

Data Research Africa in Durban – with Mathabo Malepe of the LAPC – were responsible for the overall management of the research and reports. So thanks too to Aki Stavrou, Julian May, Laura Bedford and Justine Burns.

The people who read and commented on the first, somewhat sketchy draft of *Down to Earth*, should be profusely thanked. They were William Beinart, Rosalie Kingwill, Wim van Averbeke, Joanne Yawitch and Simon Forster.

Their many criticisms and equally numerous ideas were invaluable and, since they were taken very seriously, created a massive amount of work. New chapters were written and commissioned, and several 'old' chapters were extensively reworked, joined, shortened or lengthened. Without their intellectual input, *Down to Earth* would not be nearly as good.

Finally – and personally – I would like to thank Indicator Press's Rob Evans for his superb design of the book and his extremely hard work, and the Indicator Press staff for their help and patience in managing the book process and dealing with the many changes needed.

CONTENTS

DOWN TO EARTH
Land Demand in the New South Africa

PART TWO STRUCTURAL CONSIDERATIONS

PART THREE POLICY

INTRODUCTION

Land is conceived in diverse and often incompatible ways by the various sectors of our society. The concerns of those who have landed interests or are interested in land do not derive from any inherent quality in the object itself, but rather from need as well as the socially and legally defined rights which have historically been attached to it.

> In many developing countries property arrangements on the land are evidently important and openly contested

In societies where land rights have been settled in favour of one segment of society or another, property relations and land seem relatively unimportant. The invariably unequal way land is distributed tends to be regarded as unchangeable and inevitable, a 'statement of fact', a 'natural order' which, when contested, is generally challenged from the fringes of the society and body politic.

By contrast, in many developing countries – including ours – property arrangements on the land are evidently important and openly contested. Social processes are incomplete and, while some ideologies are more dominant and mobilise more authority than others, none holds absolute sway.

Exploring demand for land in South Africa at the end of the 20th Century and the beginning of a new democratic order compresses the past into the present. It is a summation of the processes of an uneven and entangled transition from pre-capitalist to capitalist society, as the richly developed historical scholarship of the past 25 years reveals.

The issues of land use and access, private and communal tenure, state control and chiefly allocation, competing and conflicting interests between rich and poor – overlaid by the transition from predominantly agriculturally based societies into a single industrially based economy – have been played out in various parts of the country in different ways over the past two centuries and more.

Their outcomes were shaped and reshaped by the changing relationships between the state, different segments of capital and transforming indigenous African societies.

The standardising and monopolising effects of colonial rule and mineral led industrialisation were everywhere tempered by the diversity, complexity, resilience and flexibility of pre-existing societies. For all that, the process of protracted, often violent change transformed the countryside. It unravelled the social fabric of indigenous agrarian based societies, fundamentally affecting black people's access to and use of land.

Understanding the complexities of modern day relations on the land is more than an update of things past and is not solely undertaken for the purposes of historical redress – as important as redress is.

Rather, in establishing how land fits in with the way people live and work in our contemporary society, the foundation is laid for taking the present into the future, helping direct and find answers to the role that land can play in addressing the pressing development needs of the millions of people living in rural and urban South Africa.

This opportunity is provided by the uniqueness of the moment. For the first time in South African modern history, profound changes have brought to power a democratic government committed to reforming landed relations in order to redress the injustices of racist exclusions and to stimulate a development process which considers and is responsive to the needs of the poor.

Down to Earth reveals the urgency of a multi-lateral land and development policy which looks for answers to the land needs of our society

Down to Earth is a book about the demand for land in South Africa. It is a study of contemporary interests in land and the structural and systemic considerations which are likely to affect policy efforts to meet land needs.

It uncovers socially layered, mixed interests in and use of land which often pull in different directions, which frequently are conflictual and which invariably are difficult to resolve.

It exposes the condition of the contemporary countryside, and especially the fact that a large section of the rural population has little or no link with agricultural production. And it reveals the urgency of a multi-lateral land and development policy which looks within and especially beyond agriculture for answers to the complex and varied land needs of our modern day society.

The book brings together the findings of the national investigation into land demand which was undertaken over a two year period, starting in February 1994, by the Land and Agriculture Policy Centre (LAPC) under the auspices of its Land Reform Research Programme.

The book brings together the findings of a national, two year investigation into land demand

The study was conducted in all nine provinces by multi-sectoral research teams. As a strategic, transdisciplinary research initiative, it was built around participative, qualitative methods which were consciously aimed at widening the social base that contributes to the production, dissemination and use of knowledge.

At the same time, traditional survey techniques were used to collect quantitative information, although only limited use of the questionnaire involved has been made in the book. This information is complemented by data provided by the Central Statistical Service's October Household Survey (1995) and the Southern African Labour and Development Research Unit's Poverty Study (1994).

Inexperience, combined with an under-estimation of the training and management required to undertake such a challenging research approach – this was the first national land research project – inevitably produced mixed results.

While the national project proved to be an important learning experience, the unevenness of the results it generated is recognised by the researchers and the authors of *Down to Earth* as a limitation on the findings. As ground breaking as they are, no claim is made to present findings that are comprehensive of the subject matter or definitive on the specific issues that are tackled.

Rather, and in keeping with the fluidity of land and its reform context, what needs to be stressed is the importance of treating the research and its analysis as work in progress – as a contribution to ongoing debate, organisation and action around land and its role in development and democracy.

The book begins by exploring, in Chapter One, what is meant by land demand and what people want land for. Chapters Two to Eight concentrate on discovering who wants land or is interested in land reform, exploring a stratified land need which is differentiated by cross-cutting class, gender, colour and locality considerations. The second section of the book, Chapters Nine to Twelve, looks at the structural and systemic factors – both physical and social – which affect land need and usage. Chapters Thirteen to Fifteen explore the policy framework developed by the Department of Land Affairs, set within the context of the new Constitution and against a consideration of tenure issues. Finally, Chapter Sixteen sums up the main findings.

Tessa Marcus authored Chapters One, Four, Five, Six, Seven, Eight, Thirteen, Fifteen and Sixteen. Kathy Eales wrote Chapters Two, Three, Nine and Eleven. Adèle Wildschut wrote Chapter Twelve, and co-authored Chapter Eleven with Saliem Fakir and David Cooper, while Peter Rutsch contributed Chapter Fourteen.

Down to Earth, as an LAPC undertaking, draws on the collective intellectual effort of all the people who participated in the LAPC study into land demand, as well as those who have contributed to developing the policy context and framework for land reform. While every effort has been made to reflect or account for their ideas, responsibility for the views expressed rests with the authors.

PART ONE
DEMAND

CHAPTER ONE

DEMAND FOR LAND

One way to pose issues of land in terms of demand and supply is to make classical liberal economic assumptions the starting point of the investigation. Demand and supply presume land to be a commodity which in some way is, can, or ought to be accessed through the market.

> The demand for land encompasses people in a range of social strata, who need it for a range of reasons

In this framework, there is a given quantity of land and a given quantity of demand for land, and they somehow need to be reconciled. The problem is that while the absolute volume of land supply is quantifiable and fixed, its relative availability and usage are far less static because these are aspects of the land question which are largely socially determined.

On the demand side, quantifying the need for land is completely elastic and flexible. Its fixed character is mere illusion. It is a need which is constrained or facilitated by existing social and institutional realities and therefore may or may not be articulated, let alone addressed.

It is also important to bear in mind that intrinsically, market relations are not primarily about meeting people's needs. They are about making profit, which means meeting demand for consumption – a demand which sometimes coincides with people's needs, but often does not. The challenge, then, is to organise extra-market realities in a way that helps limit poverty.

Demand for land needs to be approached differently. Rather than being part of a supply equation which assumes a market relation, demand for land can be explored in terms of social needs.

This perspective gives rise to a whole set of alternative questions about who needs land, what they need land for, how they locate land in relation to other needs, and how they are organised around land need. They are, in fact, questions about social relations and how different classes and strata relate to one another. They precede and determine what 'supply and demand' will look like and what their social outcomes may be. It is this approach which will be used to inform discussion of land demand in contemporary South Africa, both to get a sense of who wants land for what, and to understand the strengths and limitations of market mechanisms in realising needs.

> *"People have different interests in land, and make different claims to rights in land. They often want land for a plurality of reasons. A piece of land can be a place to farm, somewhere to keep cattle or to come back to, a source of security or a stake in the community."* (Francis and Williams 1992)

There is a demand for land in South Africa. It is a demand which encompasses people in a range of social strata, who need it for a range of reasons.

To understand land needs this chapter will focus on the kinds of demands for land that have been articulated, and especially on interest in residential land, historical rights, and production. There is also an intrinsic institutional interest in land in the traditional authorities system – broadly defined to include the management systems created in the Coloured Reserve Areas – which needs to be understood.

In subsequent chapters, where the relation will be turned around to focus on who has landed interests and/or is interested in land, this complex issue will be explored in detail – especially with respect to agricultural production and the social relations related to it.

Residential land

Socially and geo-physically, the most universally articulated demand is for residential land. With the exception of some remote rural settlements, rural and urban people everywhere want land on which to live.

The most universally articulated demand is for residential land

Their need for residential land reflects the legacy of restricted land access to black people bequeathed by apartheid. But it also reflects other general social processes and trends, including ongoing restructuring of commercial agriculture, demographic transition, generalised urbanisation, and a weak set of social welfare institutions.

The biggest need is for new residential land. It is a need most strongly expressed by people who have recently entered the overcrowded informal and township settlements of service centres, rural towns and black freehold tenure areas, or are occupying commonage or municipal land for want of a place to stay.

The demand for residential land is intimately tied up with tenure security

Many of these new urban residents are retrenched farm workers expelled off commercial – white owned – farm land. Over the past decade, there has been a marked shrinkage in absolute levels of full-time employment on farms in all parts of the country except the Western Cape.

Others come from rural areas adjacent to settlements. Many of these new entrants have not been allocated sites because there is no land available and because they cannot afford to buy a site. Invariably, they are forced to squat on other people's land, adding to an already burgeoning 'back yard' tenant population.

Farm workers who are still employed express a strong desire for a residential site off the farm, in nearby towns or villages. Essentially they hope to reduce their dependence on their employers and give themselves some security and a place to live, should they be retrenched.

There is a demand for new land for residential purposes which is generational and comes from the needs of young families beginning new households.

In addition to new sites, there is some demand for additional land from people with residential property. Many people moving into urban settlements have been allocated plots which are smaller than they are used to and are often inadequate for the living space their households need. Others want to garden their sites to supplement food and income. This ties in with the shift away from arable field cultivation to home gardens noted, for example, in the Eastern Cape.

Another demand for residential land centres around security. Tenant relations everywhere are insecure. There is a dearth of enforceable law and practice which sets standards and protects tenant rights, making most tenants subject to the vagaries of their landlords.

With the possible exception of land in communal areas of the former homelands, the demand for residential land is intimately tied up with tenure security. This is often expressed as a desire for freehold rights because of historically bad relations between tenants and private landlords, and tenants and different levels of the state.

Claiming restitution

Land claims which arise out of historical dispossession are the most strongly organised demand. People in every province have been affected by and lost land to racially defined and colonially driven land expropriation. Presently, despite the socially disintegrating effects of forced removals, there are communities and individuals across the country who are laying claim to their lost land.

Table 1: Claims lodged with the Land Claims Commission (March 5, 1996)

Province	Rural	Urban	Total
Western Cape	49	1 791	1 840
Eastern Cape	165	203	368
Northern Cape	102	27	129
Free State	59	0	59
KwaZulu-Natal	736	1 748	2 484
Mpumalanga	273	11	284
Northern Province	351	13	364
Gauteng	223	941	1 164
North West	165	37	202
Total	**2 123**	**4 771**	**6 894**

Source: Commission on Restitution of Land Rights (1996)

Socially, restitution claims are not homogeneous, either in terms of the interests laying claim to land or the parties against whom claims are being made. In this they reflect the multi-lateral and multi-layered impact of dispossession.

Communities claiming land vary in size, social organisation and institutional capacity. They reflect a range of tenure systems including communal, freehold, leasehold, labour tenancy and traditional tenure, often in combination. Their claims for restitution are specific and various, arising from different kinds of dispossession instituted at different stages over the past eight decades.

Land claims which arise out of historical dispossession are the most strongly organised demand

In Mpumalanga, for example, claims are being lodged by chiefs on behalf of followers who lost land as a result of the creation of bantustans. Both there and in Northern Province, others are claiming land lost to state and private nature reserve initiatives.

In the former homelands there are numerous land claims being made around land lost through state imposed ‘rehabilitation’ and 'betterment', for example in the Eastern Cape and Northern Cape. In the coloured reserves of the Northern Cape, claims are being made against land lost through forced privatisation.

> Claims for restitution of urban residential land are the most numerous, because most are lodged individually

African freehold communities are claiming land lost through 'blackspot' removals, for example in the Free State, Mpumalanga and KwaZulu-Natal. In both of the latter provinces, labour tenants are in conflict with white farmers over historical land rights.

And everywhere there are claims for restitution of urban residential land which arise out of the implementation of the Group Areas Act. They are generally the most numerous, because most are lodged individually.

They also predominate in some provinces – for example in Gauteng, the Western Cape and the Free State – because of specific features of the urban-rural profile or because of the weight of a metropolitan centre where Group Areas Act provisions affected a large number of people, as in Durban in KwaZulu-Natal.

Most of the restitution claims are being made against the state, although there are claims which are directed at multiple parties to include the state as well as private individuals and institutions. There are also restitution claims directed against individuals, for example by labour tenants against white farmers, although in rural areas they appear to be a minority. For example, the case study of 18 contemporary land claims and conflicts in KwaZulu-Natal found that less than a quarter were directed against white farmers.

Restitution claims, although strongly and widely articulated, are contained. In part this is because claims are directed at specific pieces of land. But in part it is because of the parameters that policy sets up around the process – the definitions of who is eligible, under what circumstances and within which time frame. These rules are designed to make the process as manageable and finite as possible. It is an approach to policy which may work, although there are tensions which may upset the process.

Presently, the rules exclude individuals and communities who, for example, may have strongly felt grievances about dispossessions that predate 1913 or whose aboriginal title is not recognised in the current definition, as in the case of Namaqualanders in the Northern Cape. However, these cases can be considered by the Minister of Land Affairs on request. Communities which are not well organised may not be able to meet deadlines set for submitting their claims.

But perhaps most problematic are the long term consequences of conflict that may be generated by the claiming process itself. Invariably, land being claimed is already occupied. It may also be claimed by more than one community, against more than one party.

The potential for generating disputes – the permutations of which are many and varied – is enormous. Restitution may give rise to endemic and protracted conflict which would inevitably prolong and complicate what was envisaged as a limited short term measure to redress historical injustice. These issues are compounded by the number of claims and the limited institutional capacity to process them quickly.

Land for production

There is a demand among segments of the rural population for land for production purposes. The strongest and most widespread demand is for arable fields and gardens.

It is a demand which comes from a large proportion of landless people, located in all parts of the countryside, including on white owned commercial farms and in rural service centres, villages and towns. It is also an expressed need of people who presently access some arable allocations within former reserves, on freehold and mission land.

Men, and especially women, express an interest in getting and using land for cultivation. The principal motivation for most people to grow crops is their drive to supplement household food supplies and, where possible, to supplement household incomes through the sale of surpluses.

Given structural and high rates of cyclical unemployment as well as endemic poverty in all rural areas throughout South Africa, this demand is not surprising. The majority of rural households experience intermittent periods when they do not have enough food, while a substantial and fluctuating minority never have enough. Accessing new or getting more arable land is a livelihood strategy which they hope will help alleviate their problems.

People are interested in getting land to supplement household supplies

In general, commercial small scale surplus and micro producers tend to put agricultural land to similar patterns of usage in each of the provinces, although they operate at significantly different scales and within significantly different land, labour and capital parameters. Thus, within the generalised demand for arable land, there are also indications of specification, hesitation and concerns which arise from agro-ecological and social trends.

Micro and small surplus producers have been hit by drought, adverse terms of trade, theft and residential encroachment

Under the impact of sustained and unremitting drought many households, who may have planted in the past, have not been able to do so. Others still able to cultivate – for example in KwaZulu-Natal and the Eastern Cape – appear to be adopting production strategies which are more risk averse, including reducing the costs of inputs and services and limiting the commitment of household labour. The interest in household gardens and some tendency to move away from field crop production underscores this trend.

The more cautious approach to field cropping is also evident among relatively well placed commercial producers who are pressured by the combined effect of drought, a shift away from 'preferential sector' government policies and adverse terms of trade. In the Free State, for instance, farmers have moved away from cultivating marginal arable lands, reverting to less expensive and less labour intensive pastoral operations.

Theft is another constraint which adversely influences cropping and land use intensity. Although not confined to small scale surplus producers or to arable production in general, crop producers in some parts of the country are particularly hard hit.

In communal areas in former Ciskei, for example, producers identified theft as one of the main reasons mitigating against continued involvement in field cultivation. The negative cyclical impact is that, as small producers leave, those who remain become more vulnerable and less inclined to produce, accelerating the decline in land use and aggravating household food security.

Arable and grazing land which is presently accessed by black people is threatened almost everywhere by residential encroachment. In most communal and freehold – 'blackspot' – areas it has become impossible to allocate new households arable and/or grazing land. This applies to new settlers as well as to new generation households within communities. The situation is such that, most often, land is taken out of productive use in order to accommodate people's need for living space.

Coming from a different direction, black land access has been squeezed by the combined effects of racial policies and commercialisation. For example, municipal commonage outside homelands and communal land in homelands has been leased to white farmers or taken over by agricultural parastatal organisations for high technology, capital intensive, cash crop production schemes.

Communal land – commonage

Communal access is not confined to the former homelands. In many towns throughout the country, land has been set aside for common access by inhabitants, usually to graze stock and less often for cultivation. This land is usually called commonage and, for example, is found surrounding most small towns in the western half of the Eastern Cape.

Since the establishment of the towns, municipal regulations have controlled the use of commonage. Initially this meant that inhabitants of a town were allocated grazing rights, which were determined by an individual's residential status in the town. A nominal fee was charged.

Most black and coloured people, by virtue of residing in 'native locations', were excluded from using commonage and prohibited from keeping stock without special authority. A few people of colour who owned property in town were exempted from these restrictions. Some others were allowed to run a few stock for a small fee, a practice which may have occurred at times when the carrying capacity of the commonage exceeded the number of white owned stock.

However, by the early 1970s all the commonage land of all the towns in the Eastern Cape study area had been leased out to white farmers. Currently, commonage is leased or sold to white farmers only, as over the years legislative mechanisms have made it easier for local authorities to dispose of commonage land.

Clearly, regulations developed over time entrenched practices which favoured enfranchised white inhabitants at the expense of disenfranchised black and coloured people. Not surprisingly, this is currently a bone of contention

Black land access has been squeezed by racial policies, commercialism and exclusion from municipal commonage

People's interest in land for grazing raises different sets of questions. There is a need for grazing land and an articulated demand for livestock which is especially, but not entirely, expressed by men. This is not surprising, since most rural communities in southern Africa developed historically around pastoralism.

On the one hand, the present situation reflects the legacy of dispossession and the demise of pastoral conditions which prevailed until the beginning of the 20th Century. Today many rural

Racial and commercial encroachment on commonage

Aberdeen in the Eastern Cape is a good example of racial and commercial discrimination on commonage. Aberdeen's commonage consists of 4 500 hectares surrounding the town.

For many years a section of the commonage – '*die houtbos*' – was used for fuelwood collection by residents of Lotusville, the coloured township. The area was declared a nature reserve by the municipality in 1973. Access to fuelwood was denied, causing hardship for many households.

The bulk of the Aberdeen commonage is rented to white farmers for grazing, while the remainder is used for the nature reserve, an airfield, a golf course and a dump. Blacks and coloureds are not allowed to graze stock, and they have to keep their goats in their backyards.

This is a sore point. They feel that white farmers have been favoured and that the municipality has never taken the trouble to evaluate the competence of 'location farmers'. The Lotusville Men's group, consisting mainly of former farm workers, are well aware of the need for careful management so as not to degrade sensitive grazing grounds (James *et al* 1995).

After decades of dispossession there is a need for grazing land and a demand for livestock

households no longer keep livestock, apart from a handful of chickens. Of those who do have animals, most keep a few pigs, goats and cattle, although the number of animals held by households varies between communities and regions. Of those with livestock, in nearly every community studied across the country only a tiny minority have holdings of any scale.

On the other hand, the legacy of pastoralism persists. It is expressed in various ways, perhaps most strikingly in the retention of livestock by households under the most adverse conditions. When all efforts to access grazing land fail, many people leave their animals to roam between houses in dense urban settlements.

For many households, livestock holdings are an asset which keeps alive their connections with rural roots and culture. This suggests that livestock, and particularly cattle, are not simply commodities.

The 'cattle mystique' attributed to Africans reflects, rather, the heritage of pre-capitalist relations in which stock are very much like land: a multi-purpose utility addressing a range of physical and social needs in complex ways. Moreover, the way stock are kept and used is often very different from a commercial production system, as irksome as it may be for development experts and commercial farmers who understand production in a very specific way.

It has been suggested that, for most communal systems, livestock are more a subject than an instrument of nature. Cattle are harvested rather than produced, with minimal intervention to increase productivity. In the Eastern Cape, for example:

> *"...the only widespread interventions are the kraaling of animals at night (done primarily for reasons of security) and the (externally imposed) compulsory dipping programmes, which are relatively well adhered to.*
>
> *"The communal livestock farmer doesn't plan a fodder flow programme, based on veld management and supplementation (licks, animal feeds, forage production). August and September are the dying months for cattle and sheep. Goat mortalities are low...Traditionally, arable land becomes part of communal grazing land."* (Van Averbeke and De Lange 1995)

While livestock belong to and represent a major asset in individual rural households, the system built around harvesting presumes commonage. It is communal access to and use of land that has enabled many of those who still run stock to keep them.

The only exceptions are labour tenants and some farm workers who have been allowed to run a limited number of cattle, sheep or goats on the farms where they live or with the owner's herds – but always on terms set by the owners.

The African 'cattle mystique' reflects a heritage in which stock are a multi-purpose utility addressing a range of needs

The need to access land communally in order to continue to run livestock is part of the reason why residents in the Coloured Reserve Areas of the Northern Cape have resisted past efforts to privatise. It is also why township residents and commercialising producers are formally and informally claiming back the commons.

The relatively less urgent demand for grazing land generated by the survey, therefore, needs to be treated with some caution, not least of all because it may be that people who want to keep livestock traditionally, consider grazing land to be a matter of the community and not something to be addressed by individuals.

The advantages of communal grazing systems are not lost to commercialising black farmers either, whose capital base is often weak and whose rates of profitability are low. Using both systems, they are able to offset costs and enhance profits.

The unexpectedly low articulated demand for grazing land may well reflect the decimating effects of drought, which in 1992 saw the loss of 243 000 large and 107 000 small stock units in the communal sector. Stock will increase again, and there is strong evidence that people are beginning to rebuild their holdings – for example, in KwaZulu-Natal. But the recovery process is still at an early stage.

Communal access to and use of land has enabled many who still run stock to keep them

The demand for grazing land may also be indicative of the tendency for stock holding to concentrate in the hands of a few, which would effectively limit a generalised demand for more grazing land to an elite minority.

At a very general level, there are clearly different tendencies regarding the kinds of tenure relations which are appropriate to arable and pastoral production. When it comes to grazing land, communal tenure dominates and is a preference expressed even by commercialising producers. When it comes to arable production the situation is less clear, with an interest in freehold tenure being most strongly expressed by commercialising producers while micro and some surplus producers favour communal arrangements.

Land in Thaba Nchu

In the past Agricor accessed land for agriculture in the former homelands through project farming. Resource poor farmers, who were allocated land by the local headman, hired Agricor to undertake all agricultural operations on their land. At the end of the season Agricor paid them after deducting costs.

The system was discontinued in the early 1990s because it resulted in significant financial losses to Agricor, as well as engendering a culture of dependence among communities.

The problem of lack of resources for inputs continues to exclude most community members from farming. In practice only a few local people cultivate their land.

Otherwise arable lands in South Africa's Development Trust areas are often hired from those who have nominal rights by individual farmers who do have the resources for inputs. Trust village lands are also hired by 'outsiders', who own tractors and have spare capacity.

Communal land for mining

In Vioolsdrift, in the Northern Cape, commonage has been used for mining. The Vioolsdrift Commonage was proclaimed specifically for use by the coloured population. Traditionally the people of the area have been successful goat farmers, and the land would have been used for grazing.

In the late 1980s and early 1990s, assistance was given to the coloured people of the Vioolsdrift-Steinkopf area by Lanok – *Landelike Ontwikkelings Korporasie*, a creation of the House of Representatives – to develop small scale mining. Although it was perceived by the then government that this would be a more lucrative form of land use than keeping stock, Lanok failed to develop small scale miners. It appears that most participants were not ready or committed to taking on such a highly technical operation.

At present the Commonage is being used by a few small scale mining companies. Applications for mining rights and surface rights used to be granted by local management councils. Now, to start mining on the Vioolsdrift Commonage, an application has also to be made to the Department of Land Affairs and a rehabilitation plan compiled.

Conclusion

There is evidence that, in most parts of the country, there is a need for and an interest in land. Land physically locates people's sense of being – past and present. For many, interest in land is simply for residential purposes. But for a substantial minority, in addition to being a place to live, land has potential productive value which households can use to help make a living.

There is a preference for communal tenure over grazing land, but interest in both communal and freehold tenure over arable land

The issues of who has interests in and wants to use land in a socially differentiated countryside are addressed next. Although people are divided into discrete categories, in fact conditions in the countryside are very complex and diverse. Many people fall between categories. For example, there are farm workers who also have access to communal land and farm as micro producers.

Also, even when people fall into categories, they are often physically located in the same area and work together under the same conditions. For instance, in any one community there are likely to be many landless people, micro producers, an elite of surplus producers, and people from all these categories who work in commercial agriculture and elsewhere. But among all this diversity clear trends are evident, as will be shown in the following chapters.

CHAPTER TWO

QUANTIFYING RURAL PROBLEMS

The government has committed itself to targeting land reform at the poorest of the poor. Information collected from LAPC research undertaken at provincial and sub-regional levels indicates emphatically that nationally, the poorest of the poor are female headed, landless households.

> The poorest of the poor are female headed, landless households

Yet the bald statistics of the Land Reform Research Programme's national survey can convey little of the texture of rural poverty, beyond the gross indicators of insufficiency, unemployment and landlessness.

Household coping strategies and people's perceptions of choice and opportunity are not reflected in the data, nor are the processes of decision making or who makes decisions.

There are thriving settlements of small scale farmers, who produce saleable surpluses and will compete successfully in any market. They are a small minority, mostly men, and invariably they have access to off-farm incomes.

There is a broad stratum of people with access to one or more hectares of land, who produce almost exclusively for their own consumption.

And then there is a large underclass of people, barely afloat, with little or no land, no secure housing, little education and very few prospects.

Some indicators from the LAPC research are combined here with data from the two most recent comprehensive baseline surveys: the Central Statistical Service's 1995 October Household Survey and the Southern African Labour and Development Unit's Poverty Study 1994, as well as from other sources.

Land Reform Research Programme database

Using a combination of detailed district studies and statistical appraisals, the Land Reform Research Programme was an ambitious attempt to develop a demographic and socio-economic profile of potential land reform beneficiaries at a national level, using a combination of quantitative and qualitative research methods.

The programme's database (Attwood *et al* 1995) was built from more than 2 000 responses to closed-ended structured questionnaires collected in 61 case study areas.

Working with a range of techniques which favoured extensive participation by informants and skills development within the field research teams, the surveys covered an ambitious range of questions. In the final analysis, the value of the overall findings is qualified by internal methodological problems and questions of consistency, selection of respondents and weighting of settlement types.

Given the different approaches to sample design, it is impossible to view the data as representing the country as a whole: at best, it offers an indication of trends. Still, the findings do afford a unique glimpse of the attributes, needs and aspirations of a wide range of rural people who have rarely been consulted for policy purposes before.

Fieldwork was conducted by 14 field research teams between November 1994 and March 1995. Respondents were overwhelmingly mature adults, half of whom were selected from case study areas and the balance from other areas to cover people not involved in participatory research processes.

The average age of respondents was 46 years, and the median age 44 years. Fewer than 1% of respondents were younger than 18 years. Women respondents outnumbered men by 59:41.

Respondents identified their settlement types in the following proportions: tribal authority areas (30%); formal townships (25%); shanty areas (15%); villages (8%); freehold areas (7%); and farms (7%).

Limited resources meant that the data was not weighted to be nationally representative, nor was the sample in each province weighted to represent the overall proportion of each province's population to the national population, nor was it weighted to reflect the proportion of each kind of settlement found nationally.

In 1994 there were about 3,6 million black rural households

Table 2: Breakdown of interviews by province (1995)

Province	Sample %	Total Sample Size	Number of Case Study Areas	Minimum Sample/ District	Maximum Sample/ District
Eastern Cape	15	306	10	1	100
Mpumalanga	7	150	12	1	44
Free State	13	276	10	10	50
Gauteng	5	100	11	1	33
KwaZulu-Natal	20	424	8	11	161
North West	12	242	3	79	82
Northern Cape	5	100	3	33	34
Northern Province	10	210	2	74	136
Western Cape	14	290	2	126	164
Total	101	2 098	61		

Source: Attwood *et al* (1995). National Report Vol 1. LAPC Land Reform Research Programme.

There is no longer any clear demarcation between residential and agricultural land

Baseline indicators

❐ Population pressure and land use

Widely differing data sources make it difficult to analyse the available demographic data with any confidence. The most recent figures suggest that in 1994 there were about 3,6 million black rural households. This population may be expected to change over time due to countervailing forces: natural increase, migration to urban industrial centres and the unquantifiable impact of AIDS.

The present, overall trend of growth in the number of black rural households of about 1,02% a year suggests there will be about 4,2 million black rural households by the year 2006.

Population growth between the census years of 1985 and 1993 shows wide regional variation: for example, 0,79% for the Northern Cape and 3,95% for Northern Province (Development Bank of Southern Africa 1994). The impact of this growth on natural resources varies accordingly.

In many places, the demise of effective local administrative systems, coupled with population growth, has meant there is no longer any clear demarcation between residential and agricultural land. The result is a growing tendency for people to build houses on farm land

(Wood *et al* 1995). This is particularly so in peri-urban settlements, where shack farming is a lucrative form of land use.

There is clearly an urgent need for integrated development planning, with settlement patterns and farming areas planned and administered in an holistic and coordinated manner (De Wet and van Averbeke 1995). High population density *per se* does not necessarily imply acute pressure on available resources (ARDRI *et al* 1995), if land is properly planned and administered and servicing is adequate. But without good resource management strategies, long term environmental degradation is inevitable.

The paucity of alternatives for income generation means that rural people are placing undue pressure on the land, giving rise to over stocking, soil exhaustion and erosion.

Grossly inappropriate land use plans introduced with 'betterment' schemes – the forcible replanning of people's settlement and land use patterns in the former bantustans – aggravated these problems. Sheet erosion and widening dongas are the most obvious indicators of damage: perhaps more serious is the cumulative impact on river catchment systems and the steady silting of water courses in a largely arid country.

Demand for rural land

Based on the Land Reform Research Programme's provincial samples, 67,7% of South Africa's black rural households desire farm land. The demand for land is related to how much land one already has: those with a small amount – less than one hectare – want less than those with no land or those with more than one hectare.

This tentatively suggests different motivations for wanting farm land. Those with none to begin with want it in order to meet welfare needs, while those with relatively large amounts seek it for more commercial purposes. Most people have very little land to begin with: 55% of the bottom three fifths of the sample reported having no access to farm land, and 28% had less than one hectare.

Lack of income forces rural people to place undue pressure on the land

Most people want small amounts of land: 48% of those wanting farm land want one hectare or less. Although the overall mean demand for land is 13,3 hectares, this is skewed by the expressed demand of a few people for very large amounts of land. Men respondents

Demand for land - words of caution

The LAPC finding that 67,7% of black rural households desire farm land needs to be viewed with caution, as it reflects problems in the way questions were posed and how the data was collected and analysed.

The basic question on land demand linked land demand to agricultural activities. Thus the analysis of the nature of demand for land was biased in favour of agricultural production, and did not address demand for land for other purposes.

Compounding these problems were discrepancies in the way the survey was administered. 'Farming' was not defined, questions were interpreted in different ways by different fieldworkers, and some research teams modified the questionnaire. The sample group was small, and frequently unrepresentative. For these reasons, the quantitative data on demand for farm land has limited value.

The qualitative data, on the other hand, was unequivocal. Intense and in-depth discussions in 61 case study communities indicated that secure access to residential land was a priority, with access to additional land for farming a far lesser concern outside small scale cultivation for home consumption.

The apparent discrepancy between the qualitative and quantitative data on the nature of demand for land raises important policy questions. Once people's need for residential land has been satisfied, with access to small plots for food gardens, what importance will then be attached to land for farming? What is the scale of this 'latent' demand for land?

The average amount of land desired per household – 13,3 hectares – is disproportionately influenced by the demands of a small number of people for large amounts of land. In fact, about 25% of people want less than half a hectare of 'farm' land.

An additional 23% want between half a hectare and one hectare, and 17% want between one and two hectares. These are extremely modest demands. But cumulatively, on a national scale, they are significant.

Most people want small amounts of land: 48% of those wanting farm land desire one hectare or less

want far more land than women respondents: nearly six times more. Proposed usage of land strongly supports cultivation and gardening.

Available information indicates that around 85% of rural African households have a monthly income of less than R1 500, and are therefore eligible for the Settlement Grant. Extrapolating this proportion for the whole rural black population, the total eligible population is 3,08 million households. If 67,7% of these households desire farm land, the total number of eligible households desiring farm land could total 2,08 million.

If these figures are combined with the land demand estimates provided in the provincial surveys, the total number of farm land hectares demanded is in the order of 23,5 million – 24% of the total farm land area.

❒ Household size and composition

The average household size revealed in the LAPC research programme national survey was 6,8 members, with a very slight predominance of female household members: 52% to 48%. When considering gender alongside age, the data shows that among children (one to 15 years), the gender split is almost equal. But as the ages of household members increase, so does the proportion of females: among household members aged 16 to 60 years, 53% were female and 47% male, and among those aged over 60 years, 55% were female and 45% were male.

As might be expected, there is a significant correlation between the number of household members under the age of 20 and household poverty levels. Younger households tended to be poorer than those with a larger number of adult members. Similarly, the top income groups have, on average, smaller households than those in the bottom income grouping.

Given the dearth of secondary schools in many rural areas, rural youths often complete their schooling in the larger urban areas, straddling the different worlds of urban and rural life. This begs questions about where they locate themselves, and the employment and livelihood alternatives they see presented by their choice of location and occupation.

In the Northern Province district study areas, for example, few young people were interested in agriculture and the vast majority wanted urban opportunities and lifestyles. Many are not well educated enough to compete successfully for urban jobs, while their marginal role in rural economies has the potential to lead to social instability.

> The total number of households eligible for settlement grants could total 2,08 million

Too few youths were surveyed in the LAPC research programme to develop any great insight into whether people under 25 share the values and ambitions of their parents to work the land and stay in rural areas. As it is presently structured the land reform programme is unlikely to have a great deal to offer young people in the short term, with important consequences for creating a socially sustainable system of production.

Vastly improved and more relevant rural education is one of the few long term solutions (Forster 1995). In the interim, investigating the aspirations of young people in relation to land reform is an urgent research imperative to guide policy.

There are few people in rural areas with the formal skills needed to drive rural economic revival and development

❒ Education

Men are better educated than women and young people are better educated than their parents, but education levels generally are very low (Attwood *et al* 1995). If a Standard Five qualification is regarded as the minimum requirement for adult literacy, then at least 52% of the people surveyed must be regarded as illiterate. Less than 5% have post-matriculation qualifications.

Most people with tertiary qualifications have diplomas in nursing, teaching or policing. Of the 5%, half had a teaching, nursing or police diploma and just 11% – or 0,05% of adults had a university degree. A total of 13 people surveyed had agricultural diplomas.

These figures suggest a significant brain drain out of the countryside: clearly rural areas are perceived as having little to offer people with marketable skills, and those able to find more lucrative work elsewhere appear to do so. There are thus few people in rural areas with the formal skills needed to drive rural economic revival and direct locally driven development planning.

The Northern Province district studies highlighted a strong correlation between level of education, level of employment and earning potential:

- 80,8% of those who had completed some tertiary education had jobs.
- 27,1% of those who had completed their secondary education had jobs.
- 28,4% of those with a primary education had jobs.
- Those who had completed secondary education generally earned much more than those with only primary education. A quarter of people with secondary schooling but half of those with a primary education earned less than R500 a month.

Overall, 18,9% of respondents in Northern Province were in formal employment, with men outnumbering women by three to one. The only readily available local work tends to be low waged manual work on farms or mines. One teacher from the Far North commented that it was difficult to motivate pupils to complete secondary schooling when the only jobs available were manual unskilled work (Wood *et al* 1995a; Wood *et al* 1995b).

The alarming prevalence of illiteracy highlights the importance of adult basic education as a preface to farmer development programmes and in schemes aimed at stimulating rural economic revival. On the other hand, it seems that illiteracy is not necessarily a barrier to informal trade, as the poorest of the landless poor are well represented among those engaged in informal trade such as hawking and shebeens.

Virtually all respondents wanting land for agriculture expressed interest in agricultural training. Given the high level of illiteracy, training schemes will need to be very sensitive to people's education levels.

❐ Gender roles and assumptions

Women outnumber men almost universally in the rural settlements surveyed, indicating that men remain far more mobile than women and that the labour market still offers them greater opportunities. Nevertheless, migration by women is increasing. Figures from KwaZulu-Natal indicate that 27% of all employed migrants are women, and 24% of all employed women are migrants (Marcus 1995). It is not clear whether this is a national trend, although it is supported by anecdotal evidence from the district studies.

> The vast majority of women, including female household heads, feel land should not be registered in the name of a woman

Out of a global total of 2 000 respondents surveyed nationally, 28% of households were headed by women. Yet patriarchal assumptions about gender roles persist. When asked in whose name land allocations should be registered, 54% said it should be in the name of the male household head, just 12,7% favoured registration in the name of the female household head and 14,7% opted instead for the oldest male son.

The gender breakdown of those favouring land registration in the name of the female household head is even more revealing: 4% of male respondents and 20% of female respondents. Thus the vast majority of women, including female household heads, feel land should not be registered in the name of a woman.

There is a very clear division of household labour. Just 3,5% of adult men collect water, 2,4% cook, 2,9% do the laundry, 2,3% clean the house and 2,4% look after the children. Only 8,2% of adult women are involved in building and repairs.

In general, men desire almost six times as many hectares for their households as women

Although men and boys are more likely to tend livestock than women, there is little distinction when it comes to ploughing and planting. More women than men are involved in weeding and harvesting, and men are more likely than women to transport farming inputs and sell produce. Again, this suggests that men are generally more mobile than women, and certainly their low level of participation in daily household chores indicates that on the whole they can be more readily spared than women.

Gender and demand

The amount of land desired is strongly related to gender. In general, men desire almost six times as many hectares for their households as women. The practical importance of this observation is that great care must be taken at the planning stage when beneficiaries are determining how they wish to use their Settlement Grants. Left to themselves, men would allocate far more to land purchase than women would prefer.

❒ Poverty

Despite their failings, the two main headcount measures of poverty suggest that poverty is more widespread in rural areas than in urban areas. One measure found that in 1989, more than 16 million South Africans had incomes lower than the minimum subsistence level, and that 93% of them were black (Department of Agriculture 1990). Excluding the former Transkei, Bophuthatswana, Venda and Ciskei states, the same source estimates that 74% of poor black people live in rural areas.

The Urban Foundation (1991) investigated the number of people in households living below the minimum living level – R8 500 a year – and estimated that in 1990, 17,1 million people were in such households, of whom 96% were black. It estimated that twice as many poor black people lived in rural areas (11 million) than in urban areas (5,3 million). The Urban Foundation also noted that income inequality is more acute among rural black than urban black households.

Other measures of particular interest are those of nutritional status. Although the information is insufficient, it appears that the nutritional status of black rural children is far worse than that of urban black children.

The worst malnutrition indicators were found in the homelands, while the children of well established urban residents were less likely to be at risk (Macro Economic Research Group 1993). The infant mortality rates of rural African and coloured children have been estimated to be at least 2,6 times higher than those living in urban areas.

However, the degree of poverty is much more acute in some regions and some districts than in others.

Also, some households are far poorer than others, and we know that the incomes earned by black women in rural areas, or by female headed or female dominated households, are much lower than incomes earned by black men or by male dominated households.

The black rural population, which we have seen constitutes two thirds of poor black people, contains many more women than men. In rural areas as a whole in 1991, the female to male ratio was 1,06:1, while the ratio of working age adults – 20 to 64 years – was 1,38:1 (Merg 1993).

There are indications in work done by the Development Bank of Southern Africa that in the poorest rural areas, the percentage of males is even lower.

This is supported by analysis of the Saldru data, which finds that the risk of living in poverty in rural areas is larger for women than men (May *et al* 1995).

It is estimated that twice as many poor black people live in rural areas (11 million) than in urban areas (5,3 million)

Policy to tackle poverty or malnutrition will be most effective if it is aimed at specific rural households. This warrants stratified analysis of the rural population as well as use of average figures.

❒ Migrancy and employment

Among people in the economically active age group, 80% slept and ate at home every night, suggesting that roughly 20% migrate to some extent (Attwood *et al* 1995). However, the number of migrants could well be higher, since longer term migrants might not always have been counted.

Of the 20% of economically active adults frequently away from home, 6% returned during holidays, 5% returned home once or twice a month, and 3% returned home every weekend. One percent returned just once a year, and 4% returned irregularly (Attwood *et al* 1995).

Among those in the economically active age group 29% were employed, formally or informally and 25% were unemployed

While migrant labour depletes a family of labour, remittances from migrant labour stave off deeper impoverishment. Just how critical this is, is revealed in the status of households without access to remittance income.

Farm workers, for example, seldom have access to remittances, and their household income is determined primarily by the number and sex of people in full-time employment, or doing part-time or seasonal work at local wage rates (Marcus, 1995).

The absolute growth in joblessness has had a particularly severe impact on rural households who previously depended on remittances, with migrants who received formal wages increasingly having to rely on informal sector activities (Marcus 1995).

The National Report indicated that among those in the economically active age group:

- 29% were employed, formally or informally
- 9% were self employed or employed in casual labour
- 6% were engaged in farm work or house work
- 24% were scholars
- 5% were disabled or retired
- 25% were unemployed, with the vast majority actively seeking work.

Informants stressed that farm work is an option pursued almost always as a last resort. Farm workers appear to have the lowest education levels, and earn pitifully small wages. Rates of pay as low as R5 a day are not uncommon in several parts of the country, although the norm seems to lie between R150 and R350 a month.

Women are far less likely to be in paid employment and, when they are, they are paid less than men. In the Maila Mapitsane area of Sekhukhuneland, for example, no women earned more than R500, while men in formal employment earned R500 to R1 800 (Wood *et al* 1995b).

In Northern Province, women are establishing a growing presence on commercial farms as seasonal workers, and in the Western Cape this trend is well established. More men than women in the Western Cape are reported unemployed, echoing the surge in employment of women reflected in the 1991 census data, which reported a 143,7% increase since 1970 in the number of women employed in agriculture. Most are employed on a seasonal basis at lower wages – 75% on average – than the men they replaced (Wesso 1995a).

❒ Income and employment

People in rural settlements are not predominantly farmers: they engage in a range of income generating activities.

Information on income sources for rural African households is available from the Saldru survey. The Department of Land Affairs is presently using a beneficiary cut-off point set at a household income of R1 500 a month. Using the Saldru data, 85% of rural African households fall within this cut-off.

Table 3: Income data

Average for whole sample	Average for bottom 20%	Average for 21%-40%	Average for 41%-60%	Average for 61%-80%	Average for top 20%	Average for hh's with less than R1 500
R819,306	R134,18	R366.20	R571,02	R906,00	R2 126,17	R563,24

Source: Saldru (1994)

Wages and pensions are by far the most important income sources, although the precise weighting of the two depends on regional labour markets and the number of wage labourers or migrants a household is able to field. Wages are both the most common source of household income, and the source of income that usually contributes the most to overall household income.

People in rural settlements are not predominantly farmers: they engage in a range of income generating activities

The second most common and the second largest contributor is pensions and disability grants. Remittances take third place. While more households received income from other sources than from own businesses, household income from own businesses was higher on average than from other sources (Attwood *et al* 1995):

- ❑ 11% of households derive some portion of their total household income from operating a business. Of this figure, 50% earn less than R400 per month.

Table 4: Different sources of monthly household income by quintile

Household income	Wage income rands	Remittance income rands	Pensions and transfer income rands	Own business income rands	Income: other sources rands
Bottom quintile	up to 286	up to 130	up to 370	up to 100	up to 23
Second quintile	287-550	131-208	371-390	101-300	24-50
Mid-quintile	551-900	209-400	391-492	301-600	51-130
Fourth quintile	901-1 500	401-750	493-780	601-1 200	131-333
Upper quintile	1 501-44 979	751-600	781-5 000	1 201-29 000	334-5333
Median	700	300	390	400	97
Mean	1 207	501	555	1 452	311
% Households earning income	61%	22%	38%	11%	15%

Source: Attwood *et al* (1995) National Report Vol 1. LAPC Land Reform Research Programme.

Two thirds of rural people receive no income from agriculture, and roughly 85% have no cattle

- ❑ Those entirely dependent on petty trade are the most impoverished. Thus, 60% of those with access to less than one hectare or no land at all, depend entirely on businesses which generate under R200 per month. There is not a significant difference in the income of those with no land, and those with access to less than one hectare.
- ❑ 46% of households earn less than R750 from all sources.
- ❑ 44% of landless households have an income below R400 a month.

Jobs are scarce and the labour market is highly fragmented, so the poorest often engage in several forms of economic activity, including half-day work and piece work. Two thirds of the rural population receive no income from agriculture, but some of those without land are able to farm using gardens. Roughly 85% of the rural population have no cattle.

These factors emphasise the need to create other income sources and safety nets for the rural poor. The poorest groups are heavily concentrated in low paying insecure sectors of employment, such as domestic service and farm work. These are the sectors in which wage improvement will be difficult to implement in the form of minimum wage agreements, and cannot simply be left to wage agreements.

To provide greater income and security, it is necessary to expand alternative employment opportunities and to provide improved and complementary income sources.

In the face of this degree of poverty, even modest initiatives which address food security and household nutrition will be significant.

In all areas of the country, most respondents – 65% nationally – felt that poverty should be the main criterion in selecting the primary beneficiaries of a land reform initiative. But extremely low household incomes pose a profound challenge to a market based approach to land reform targeted at 'the poorest of the poor': few households will be able to contribute to the cost of land purchase or maintain loan repayments, even where substantial cash grants are made available to them by government.

What these figures also emphasise is the importance of multiple income sources in rural subsistence. Any suggestion that small scale and subsistence farmers can survive exclusively off the land is misplaced. Acknowledging this was one of the most painful lessons of Zimbabwe's land reform programme, where part-time farmers were excluded from resettlement schemes for a long time (Nyamapfene 1995).

CHAPTER THREE

RURAL AND URBAN RESIDENTIAL LAND DEMAND

The terms 'land reform' and 'rural restructuring' are often used interchangeably, in a way which conflates land, agriculture and rural areas. Yet the need for land reform encompasses considerably more than rural land for agriculture. One of the most striking features of the Land Reform Research Programme's investigation into land demand was evidence of the scale of demand for residential land.

The Land Reform Research Programme found evidence of immense demand for residential land in both rural and urban areas

This need is pressing in urban areas because of rapid growth in urban settlements and bottlenecks in the development of residential land. But it would be wrong to assume that the need for residential land is primarily an urban concern.

Displaced farm workers, refugees from violence and families who have outgrown their available accommodation are among the many seeking a place to stay away from the large towns and cities. In many existing rural settlements, overcrowding is already acute, and land better suited for other uses is being occupied by stealth or force.

Urban land demand

Influx controls were superseded in the late 1980s by a policy of regulated or 'orderly' urbanisation, but there is no longer much that is orderly about urban settlement. In Gauteng alone there is an estimated backlog of 500 000 housing units: in view of the limited resources available to them, the difficulties which the depressed small towns of the interior face in meeting the need for residential land and housing are possibly comparable.

Urban settlement seems to have followed two streams since the repeal of influx controls in 1986.

One stream was directed towards metropolitan areas, leading to a proliferation of backyard shacks and squatting on urban peripheries. Most shack residents were from existing formal townships, and were seeking to escape township regulations, rent, overcrowding and familial pressure to share their incomes (Kruger 1995).

Over the last decade, another pattern of urbanisation has emerged alongside ongoing metropolitan sprawl. Most new informal settlement has been taking place in smaller towns, with many new residents being people who were squeezed off the land, or retrenched farm workers and their families who have been displaced by drought and agricultural restructuring.

In many cases, people are simply unable to survive in the countryside, being forced by poverty and other factors to seek a home and income elsewhere. A large number of rural people have no access to arable land.

The proportion varies widely from region to region: in the Weenen-Estcourt study area of KwaZulu-Natal, for example, 61% of respondents reported no allocated arable land, compared with 30,5% in the Mhlatuze catchment study area. In a survey of communal areas in the Eastern Cape, 66% of households had no arable land and only half of households had gardens.

Many other rural households retain access to productive land, but due to a range of factors – lack of water, capital and security against theft – they are unable to generate a livelihood from it, and depend on cash incomes from other sources. When those income sources diminish people are often marooned, living on the land but unable to live from it.

Landlessness encompasses a wide range of people, from vagrants at the one extreme to farm workers on the other, whose right to a place to live usually depends on their employment status. It includes land invaders, illegal occupants and people living in overcrowded housing for lack of an alternative. It covers insecure tenure and barred access to productive land, as well as people who have been displaced by conflict or drought.

> Landlessness encompasses a wide range of people, from vagrants to farm workers

The nature of urban settlement too has become more diverse, and the rate of urbanisation seems to have escalated, although the change is hard to quantify since South Africa's official statistics are notoriously inaccurate.

More revealing are the indicators of growth in some areas: in the Free State, impelled by agricultural restructuring and redundancies on the mines, the population of Tweespruit nearly doubled between 1991 and 1994 to 7 250 residents. The rise in Dewetsdorp was even higher. Thembalethu, outside George in the southern Cape, was established in the mid-1980s. In 1991 its population was a little over 14 000: it is now estimated at 40 000.

> The rate of urban settlement has escalated. The population of some small towns has doubled in the past decade or less

The catchment of origin of new arrivals has also broadened. In Mpumalanga and Northern Province there has been a steady influx of Mozambicans, some of whom work their way towards Gauteng by finding work on commercial farms and in small towns *en route*.

In Gauteng there has been a significant rise in the number of Mozambicans living in East Rand informal settlements and new townships like Orange Farm. On the Free State side of the Lesotho border, the black population of Ficksburg has tripled over the past decade, and local informants maintain that any local development attracts thousands more people from across the border.

Urban land demand is complex and diverse. The Land Reform Research Programme highlighted several sources of demand.

Natural increase in township populations

Government has not sponsored the construction of new township housing since the 1960s, and private sector housing initiatives nationally are premised on cost recovery at the very least. The result is a critical shortage of housing nationally, with the poor bearing the brunt of homelessness.

Land delivery is essential for housing delivery. Until recently, towns were developed and settled according to racial criteria, with poverty concentrated in black settlements. Black local authorities have manifestly lacked the resources to purchase or develop new land for low income settlement. With rare exceptions, white local authorities have clung to literal interpretations of their mandate, and have echoed their ratepayers in insisting 'not in my backyard'.

In the 1990s, transitional local government structures have been so constrained by their interim status – unable to raise major loans, unwilling to undertake long term projects and vulnerable to accusations of illegitimacy at the first hint of controversy – that very little has been done to ease demand for urban residential land.

Because of stagnant public sector delivery, private sector development initiatives have borne the brunt of pent-up demand for land. South west of Johannesburg, for example, the pioneering Goldev housing development scheme has been paralysed by stage managed squatter invasions, with the result that enthusiasm for similar private sector ventures has paled.

The heart of the problem lies less with land identification than with the slow process of freeing up suitable land for new settlement initiatives.

Relief is anticipated with the Development Facilitation Act, designed to ease bureaucratic bottlenecks. However, the slow passage of the Act through the legislature has raised questions about the Government's will and capacity to use it with the urgency required to break logjams (*Business Day* December 15, 1995). Meanwhile, energy that should be put into pursuing new initiatives is being consumed by crisis management.

Urban housing options span a wide range: private ownership with title; self help schemes; renting from the municipality; squatting (usually coupled with land invasion); backyard tenancy; boarding; hostels; and 'living in the bush'.

Somewhat surprisingly, the Southern Cape district studies suggest that at least some people regard squatting as an attractive option, if not the next best thing after freehold tenure. Residents assessed the various options in terms of security, freedom, self respect and cost, and squatting ranked relatively high. For at least some on the margins of the formal economy, squatting meets their need for mobility. Squatters seem to have turned homelessness to their advantage:

> *"Squatters can choose where they will work when work is available, they are relatively free from eviction and need only invest a relatively small amount of capital to build their homes..."* (Southern Cape 1995)

The heart of the housing problem lies less with land identification than with the slow process of freeing up suitable land for new settlement

Moreover, the Southern Cape research revealed, some Mossel Bay squatters opted for land invasion rather than site and service schemes, because the former offered the option of space for food gardens and grazing.

All too evidently, squatters lack services, especially water and sanitation, and formal recognition by the authorities. Residents from one Mossel Bay squatter settlement said they wanted house numbers on their shacks as an acknowledgment of their permanence.

Urban housing options span a wide range: private ownership; self help schemes; renting from the municipality; squatting; backyard tenancy; boarding; hostels; and 'living in the bush'

Successful land invasion can offer a relatively high degree of tenure security. Sometimes the local civic leads the invasion, and sometimes maverick structures – like a youth group acting independently of its parent structure – or opportunist individuals are at the forefront.

In newly invaded areas, people tend to put up one room structures initially, and wait to see how the authorities respond. Once occupation seems accepted, some squatters maintain that they enjoy greater freedom and security than boarders and backyard tenants – and they live rent free.

By contrast, backyard tenancy appears to be very unpopular: tenants have little security and relations between landlords and tenants are often exploitative and abusive. Tenants are often compelled to pay extortionate rents, especially if they are wage earners, and some landlords expect women tenants to provide sexual favours for them. Some landlords restrict their tenants' rights to receive visitors.

Informants in the Southern Cape described themselves as 'prisoners and orphans': prisoners because they have no freedom or rights, and orphans because they have no security.

Boarders generally live in the landlord's home, and at times their situation is even less favourable than that of backyard tenants. It is not unusual for boarders to have to take responsibility for a range of domestic tasks. In the Southern Cape, the great majority of land invaders are former boarders and backyard tenants. In other parts of the country – particularly the Western Cape – former hostel residents and their families are more prominently represented.

It is important to distinguish between organised land invasion and incremental encroachment. According to a recent Urban Foundation study, there are no documented cases of a significant urban land invasion being orchestrated by people recently arrived from rural areas.

As an aside one should note that in metropolitan settlements like Alexandra, Johannesburg's most central township, it seems that a growing proportion of shack residents are non-permanent economic migrants from other regions and countries, who have no wish to invest in formal housing. Their choices pose a curious challenge to urban planners seeking to formalise and upgrade the urban landscape.

Declining viability of rural subsistence

The collapse of rural subsistence economies under the weight of overpopulation, under resourcing and institutional neglect has prompted a steady flow of people from rural to urban settlements over the past three decades. Despite influx controls which officially prevented people from moving freely outside their designated ethnic homeland, there was a significant movement from rural to urban areas within the bantustans and to urban areas outside the bantustans. People settled in bantustan towns, in peri-urban settlements in the bantustans as close as possible to metropolitan centres (Winterveld), or in bantustan towns adjacent to 'white' commercial centres (Mdantsane).

Since 1986 there has been a significant movement out of the bantustans and into more promising job centres, although settlement in bantustan towns continues. There has been a dramatic increase in shack farming around Transkei towns like Butterworth, Umtata and Cala. In Butterworth, informal settlements have developed on land zoned for industrial development, and on municipal commonage (Cala, Idutywa and Mount Fletcher). Large informal settlements are growing on the edge of major urban centres, as in Pietersburg.

> Overpopulation, under resourcing and institutional neglect has prompted a steady flow of people from rural to urban settlements over the past three decades

Similar processes have been given added and specifically directed impetus in KwaZulu-Natal with the promulgation of the KwaZulu Land Act. There, giving traditional authorities permission to sell land has resulted in the flow of people moving into traditional authority districts surpassing the intake of people into private tenure communities during the past 10 years (Cross *et al* 1995).

Restructuring in the job market

In the Free State in the late 1980s and the early 1990s there has been:

> "*...a tidal wave of unemployment on commercial farms*". (Murray 1995)

This was generated by the combined effects of drought, economic stagnation and political change and, together with already high rates of unemployment among urban residents, has been aggravated by massive redundancies in the mining industry.

Between 1991 and 1994, nearly a third of workers – 60 000 out of a total of around 160 000 – were retrenched from the Free State goldfields. Of this total, at least some retained a home base on farms, while others used their mine wages to support rural homesteads. Facing bleak prospects at home, rural people are pursuing a range of survival strategies, some of which include relocation to small towns.

> *"...unemployment on the mines and unemployment on farms has affected the same families, now concentrated in shack peripheries of the metropolitan areas and the small towns"*. (Murray 1995)

The influx of poor and unemployed people has dramatically changed the racial and socio-economic profile of many small platteland towns

Many small towns, already in economic decline, are slipping deeper into poverty with the in-migration of newcomers. This trend has become marked in the past five years.

The influx of poor and unemployed people to towns has dramatically changed the racial and socio-economic profile of many small platteland towns, and further undermined any possibility of new residents finding formal jobs.

Wesselsbron, for example, now has an estimated population of 1 250 whites and 29 000 blacks, Theunissen has 1 600 whites and 35 000 blacks, and Bitterfontein has 1 534 white and 37 000 black residents, two thirds of whom live in bitterly impoverished shack settlements (Botes *et al* 1995).

Growing off-farm settlement by farm workers

Former farm workers feature prominently among those who are both landless and unemployed. Restructuring in the agricultural sector in pursuit of greater cost efficiency and competitiveness, coupled with periods of chronic drought, has led to widespread lay-offs and evictions of farm workers.

Added to this have been shifts in commercial agriculture – from grazing to timber, from cropping to grazing etc – which have displaced many farm workers.

In the Free State alone, an estimated 250 000 farm workers and their families have been retrenched or displaced from commercial farms in the past 15 years (Botes, De Wet and Heunis 1995). While the impact in other parts of the country has not been quantified in the same way, similar trends – perhaps less acute – are evident.

Since many farm workers do not have ties to other rural areas and have no secure land rights where they work, they are a particularly insecure group. Displaced farm workers are extremely vulnerable to impoverishment, since they seldom have any capital or formal education to help them exploit new opportunities, and frequently are used to relying on their employers for housing, rations, wages and education (De Wet 1994). Murray describes the situation of former farm workers in the Free State in the following terms:

> *"They are concentrated in slums such as Botshabelo and on the edges of the small towns that service farmers throughout the highveld maize triangle. Their prospects are grim.*
>
> *Formal sector or stable employment is hopelessly beyond the reach of many of the youth. Inevitably, they prey on pensioners; they live by their wits from one day to the next; and they hone their skills as best they may in the disparate nooks and crannies of the second economy."* (Murray 1995)

The impact of agricultural restructuring has varied in accordance with local agro-climatic conditions and settlement patterns.

In parts of south eastern Mpumalanga, farm land is being sold or leased to big forestry companies. Forestry has different labour requirements to those of crop farming, and employs far fewer people (Tloolo 1995).

Displaced farm workers are extremely vulnerable to impoverishment. They often rely on their employers for housing, wages and education

In the south eastern Free State, some marginal crop lands are being converted to rangeland for livestock, and the clichéd rolling plains of the maize belt are giving way to more specialised cropping where warranted by changes in the maize price (Bedford 1995).

In farm lands bordering Lesotho and other expanses of acute poverty, stock theft and other crime is rampant: particularly in marginal farm lands and sub-regions prone to drought, farming is no longer tenable in its current form (Murray 1995; De Wet and Van Averbeke 1995). Blithe proposals that black farmers should take over white farm land in these areas miss the point that the impulses of poverty pay little regard to race.

In the southern Cape, the continuing development of capital intensive agriculture as well as recession and drought have increased the number of farm workers retrenched and evicted. Many displaced people squat on the periphery of small towns in pursuit of casual or seasonal employment.

> It would be wrong to romanticise farm employment as stable. Many former farm workers are highly mobile in their pursuit of better job prospects

Farm workers have also been displaced by pre-emptive dismissal in cases where farmers have feared the impact that new labour legislation will have on wage levels and performances. Others, anticipating the worst from the new Government's land reform policies, have chosen to minimise the possibility of land claims by cutting their staff to a minimum.

Rising cross border migration from Mozambique, Zimbabwe and Lesotho, is displacing South African farm workers in some areas. In the far Northern Province a small but growing number of (illegally resident) Zimbabweans are undercutting the wages of South African farm workers. In the Free State, farm workers in some instances are being replaced with seasonal workers from Lesotho (Murray 1995).

Inevitably, the resulting landlessness contributes to rural crime and illegal settlement. Where land encroachment occurs on the edge of urban settlements, often the fences of adjacent farms are cut, animals are stolen, and fires and dogs destroy property, grazing and livestock. Commercial farmers in the vicinity often see no alternative but to abandon their farms or sell up, leading to the loss of their skills, their workers' jobs and the produce of their farms, propelling a further downward spiral (De Wet and Van Averbeke 1995).

While it is true that some farm worker families have been on particular farms for long periods, this is by no means always the case. Indeed, it would be wrong to romanticise on-farm employment as stable and long term. Many former farm workers are highly mobile in their pursuit of better job prospects.

Retrenchment and eviction is not the only impetus for farm workers setting up home in small towns. Farm workers generally depend on their employers for both shelter and employment, and thus are highly vulnerable to shifts in their employers' labour needs. The abolition of influx controls has meant that farm workers have the option of establishing shacks in townships near their place of work.

In the Free State – and no doubt elsewhere – farm workers have acquired shacks in town to provide a base for their schoolgoing children, who are not accommodated at farm schools beyond Standard Four (Bedford 1995).

Evidence from KwaZulu-Natal highlights the importance of acknowledging different interests within the farm workforce. For example, segmentation of the workforce puts casual workers who are women hired from urban settlements in a different position to women who work as casual labourers while living with full-time farm workers on the farm.

The latter do not necessarily want to leave farms and be separated from their husbands, since this might undermine the stability of their households. Equally, living off the farm could reduce employment opportunities for the wives of full-time farm workers, as they would have to compete without advantage against casual workers drawn from the urban unemployed (Marcus 1989).

In the Border region of the Eastern Cape, farmers maintain that increasing numbers of women members of farm worker households are entering domestic employment with black families in large townships like Mdantsane and Zwelitsha. This may reflect greater prospects of mobility for women, as much as additional income generating strategies (De Wet and Van Averbeke 1995).

Township based farm workers do not necessarily live there by choice. There is evidence of a growing trend in many parts of the country of hiring both full-time and seasonal farm labour from nearby townships.

> Informal settlements on the edge of small towns are becoming an important source of farm labour. Off-farm housing adds weight to calls for secure urban residential rights

For farmers, the abolition of influx controls and stringent labour regulation has meant they are free to recruit workers from wherever they wish, and informal settlements on the edge of small towns are becoming an important source of farm labour.

These workers are paid cash only, and farmers are spared the expense of providing housing and services including electricity, water, sanitation, medical care and, for some, farm schools (Hamman 1994). This trend was noted in the Western Cape, Eastern Cape, KwaZulu-Natal, Mpumalanga, Northern Province and North West studies.

Although it is too early to say whether off-farm housing will become the norm, it adds weight to calls for secure urban residential rights and for villages where farm workers' housing rights are not contingent on the employment needs of their employer.

Tenants on black owned land

Another category of people considered landless are tenants living in former 'black spots' and on other black owned land

Another category of people considered landless are tenants living in former 'black spots' and on other black owned land. Often their insecurity of tenure is linked to the economic insecurity of the land holders.

For example, quitrent tenure – a transferable land right where a small annual rent is paid for an indefinite lease for approved farming – has survived in 'black spot' areas in the Border region of the Eastern Cape. Insecurity also exists in areas where the original land title is freehold, but the land has subsequently been used and allocated on a communal or individual basis, as in Driefontein and KwaNgema in Mpumalanga.

Rabula, in Keiskammahoek, is one of the few areas in the former Ciskei where black people held land under freehold title. Over the years, land owners at Rabula accommodated landless people settling in the area who attached themselves to the owners as labour tenants, performing tasks and services in exchange for the right to cultivate a small tract of land.

During the 1950s and 1970s, the area was subjected to 'betterment planning' and consolidation of residential land. By 1990 about 40 households, completely landless, lived there by squatting on the commonage or as tenants of freehold owners.

'Black spot' areas such as Mgwali, Heckel and Wartburg took in numerous landless people – primarily displaced farm workers – despite the constant threat of forced removal. Inevitably, there are intense conflicts between quitrenters and tenants, because the quitrenters feel they have lost control of their land.

At Hlelo, in south eastern Mpumalanga, many people left the farm they had lived on for most of the century as labour tenants when it was leased to Sappi. Former labour tenants were either relocated in housing compounds elsewhere on the farm, or opted to leave. The result was a significant movement of people towards peri-urban settlements, or to 'black spots' like Driefontein. Shack farming on the edge of towns like Amsterdam is booming, while congestion at Driefontein is seriously compromising local grazing and cropping potential (Tloolo 1995).

There is strong demand for land in these settlements. Former farm workers and tenants want secure residential sites, and some would like the chance to run stock or cultivate. Short of purchasing additional farm land, there is little prospect of additional agricultural land being found to service the settlements.

Settlement trends

The current marked exodus of people from rural areas is not infinite, but a response to very particular circumstances: widespread farm worker retrenchments linked to agricultural restructuring, drought, an absolute decline in jobs for migrant workers, and a hope that the fruits of democratic government will be more accessible in town.

The indications are that the dynamic will slow, particularly if steps are taken to address the welfare needs of the rural poor.

Already there are indications that urbanisation in the Durban Functional Region is slowing down, signalling an awareness that job prospects in the urban formal sector are poor and, perhaps, an anticipation that the RDP will bring new resources to rural areas (Alison Todes, personal comment).

Interestingly, new arrivals in small platteland towns are not only from farms and rural settlements, but from cities too. In Coligny and Zeerust in North West, local observers have noted a small recent influx of people who found that big city employment opportunities were not what they anticipated. It is not clear whether they originally came from the Coligny and Zeerust areas: certainly, the number of people employed on farms of the North West maize belt has fallen sharply in the face of high levels of mechanisation.

> The exodus of people from rural areas is a response to farm worker retrenchments, drought, a decline in jobs, and a hope that the fruits of democracy will be more accessible in town

Competing land uses

Around the country there is competition over land use between agriculture, residence, recreation, conservation and, in some areas, mining as well. With the exception of the Witwatersrand, towns generally develop around fertile settlements or along rivers, and productive agricultural land is generally one of the first casualties of urban sprawl.

It is likely that settlement on the outskirts of towns and cities will continue for some years, independent of efforts by the Department of Land Affairs and local authorities to regulate settlement within designated areas. High potential agricultural land and environmentally sensitive areas are particularly vulnerable.

Urban agriculture could offer interim relief for people newly arrived in towns who lack other work opportunities

Moreover, good agricultural land adjacent to informal settlement is being abandoned in the face of theft and other crime, and residential encroachment often follows soon afterwards. Careful planning will be needed so that good agricultural land is not lost to production by unregulated urban settlement.

In Gauteng, much of the demand for housing lies west and south west of Soweto, where it competes with agriculture and mining for priority land use.

Present local authority planning proposals emphasise more compact urban structures, urban infill and densification. This could open up opportunities for market linked agricultural development on the urban periphery (Gauteng Synthesis Report, Volume One).

Agriculture need not only be a rural activity. Urban and peri-urban environments are often suited to small scale farming, particularly where the possibility of irrigation exists.

Urban agriculture offers the further advantage of providing employment and opportunities for both subsistence and commercial production. The research reports highlighted widespread demand for land for food gardens and also, although hard to quantify, significant levels of cultivation of food gardens.

Urban agriculture could offer interim relief for people newly arrived in towns who lack other work opportunities. Julian May develops the argument:

> *"People living on the fringe are not static, and should rather be seen as being on some kind of trajectory. While they may engage in agricultural production now, changing opportunities may mean that they move onto different forms of economic activity in the future."* (May 1994)

Urban agriculture also offers very productive interim land use, until it is developed for other purposes.

Demand for recreational land should not bc subordinated to other interests. As South Africa's urban areas become more dense, the need for open green spaces for recreation is intensifying.

Land availability

Rarely is there a shortage of urban land which could be developed. Virtually every South African town has a vacant 'buffer strip' separating race based settlements proclaimed under the Group Areas Act, which could be developed for housing, recreation, business or agriculture – or a combination of them. Other categories of urban land include state land, land zoned for industry but not developed, mine owned land, and commonage.

Commonage surrounds most of the small towns of the former Cape Province, and occurs less frequently in some other parts of the country. It seems there is a widespread expectation among landless urban residents that land reform will bring restored rights to commonage.

In the past, access to the land was regulated by the white local authority, and thus local white residents enjoyed priority access. Over time the system of common pastures gave way to the practice of selling and leasing commonage land to white farmers, in response to declining demand from white urban residents for grazing for their own dairy cows and sheep (James *et al* 1995).

In the Free State, town commonage encompasses 141 640 hectares and is managed by local authorities who lease the camps out on five year contracts. Leases are decided through public auctions, and most are used for grazing land. Much Eastern Cape commonage has been sold off. In Pearston, for example, only 187 hectares remain of an original 2 547 hectares of commonage land, and the proceeds of sale have disappeared into the local authority's revenue account (James *et al* 1995).

> Virtually every South African town has a vacant 'buffer strip' or commonage which could be developed for housing, recreation, business or agriculture – or a combination of these

Although relatively few black and coloured residents have been able to make use of commonage land, its leasing and sale to white farmers is keenly resented. People want access to commonage for firewood and for grazing, as stray cattle in townships contribute to health risks and road accidents and are frequently impounded.

One should note that the need for peri-urban grazing land was expressed almost exclusively by men. Where women articulated land needs other than for residential land, it was for land for poultry farming or food gardens. Local representative structures tend to be dominated by men, and their decisions are more likely to reflect men's land needs. It is important that the different needs of men and women are acknowledged, particularly when resources for land purchase are limited (James *et al* 1995).

Unviable settlements

Not all urban areas encompass developed infrastructure, public and private investment, and developed job markets. After decades of regional planning premised on political rather than economic considerations, the former bantustans are dotted with decaying towns which were developed to service decentralisation initiatives – like Botshabelo, south of Bloemfontein.

These settlements pose a particular dilemma for developers. The state has a moral duty to address the welfare needs of its citizens, but it is debatable whether there should be additional investment in artificial settlements which were created in the name of apartheid and have no prospect of economic viability. Simply providing adequate water supplies poses a severe challenge in areas remote from pipelines or adequate catchments.

> It is important that the different needs of men and women are acknowledged, particularily when resources for land purchase are limited

Similar dilemmas are posed by dense rural settlements which are towns in all but name, like Gwili-Gwili in the Eastern Cape. Demarcating and transferring residential sites to those who need them and upgrading local infrastructure is an urgent priority, but it is unlikely that these measures will do much to address local poverty let alone help local residents pay for the new services available to them.

Conclusion

Many poor families suffering unemployment and landlessness try to reorient themselves in an urban or peri-urban – and increasing a small rural town – context where there may be opportunities for income generation in full employment, casual work or the informal sector.

The scale of demand for urban land in cities, towns and small rural towns underscores the predominance of the industrial economy and the inability of South Africa's rural areas to offer the vast majority of people living there an independent livelihood.

In harsher terms, it emphasises the importance of welfarism in the current rural redistribution initiatives, and suggests that unless a coherent rural economic development strategy is devised and implemented soon, the rural component of the land reform programme will, at best, be a holding operation: the impetus for economic recovery and regeneration in rural areas is almost entirely absent.

Urban settlement dynamics in cities and rural towns, and the range of factors underpinning urban land demand, are poorly understood.

Do urban newcomers originate from rural areas or other urban settlements? If they are from rural areas, by what process do they arrive in larger towns and cities, and over what period have they made the transition? What influences their choice of settlement? What is the relative weight of 'push' and 'pull' factors? It is all too evident that we know very little about who is moving, where, why and for how long.

Census statistics show only numerical absolutes and offer few insights into the dynamics that can help planners assess where to develop infrastructure for maximum benefit. Indeed, given the scale of human movement out of South Africa's rural areas, rural development initiatives should be paying more attention to revitalising small town economies, supporting small scale processing plants and reskilling former farm workers for urban jobs.

CHAPTER FOUR

FARM WORKERS AND LABOUR TENANTS

Farm workers make up 16,5% of the economically active population. This chapter focuses on the land interests of farm workers and labour tenants. In general, the social characteristics and position of farm workers across the country reflect the different and uneven histories and conditions of production that have developed in agriculture in and across the different provinces.

The social characteristics and position of farm workers differs across the country

Farm workers

In the Western Cape, Northern Cape and Free State, most farm workers have ceased to have peasant like connections to the land.

By contrast, in Northern Province, North West, Mpumalanga, Eastern Cape and KwaZulu-Natal, while there are many fully proletarianised workers employed in commercial agriculture, there are also substantial numbers of farm workers who continue to directly access and use land for production purposes. They do this either by drawing on landed relations through former reserves, which are external to commercial agriculture, or by accessing land in commercial agriculture through labour tenant relations.

In the Western Cape, enforcement of the Coloured Labour Preference Policy significantly influenced the racial and gender composition of the farm labour force as well as conditions of employment. Most farm workers there are coloured, with their African counterparts accommodated in separate and different physical accommodation, earning less and generally with no access to family housing, child care and recreational facilities.

Also, while women in the Western Cape – as elsewhere in the country – are disadvantaged because they are most often seasonal or casual workers, atypically there is a substantial minority of women employed full-time on farms. In all other provinces, few women are

Farm worker wages

Farm workers everywhere are interested in improving their wages and conditions of employment. Low pay is their single most urgent grievance, and it impinges on every aspect of their lives, including work performance. The main interest of those who were unemployed was to find work.

Where there are additional payments in kind – mostly rations, sometimes the right to run a fixed number of stock with the main herd, and rarely some arable land – they are usually the preserve of selected full-time male workers. The main exceptions are instances where there is communal cooking to provide for the needs of harvest workers, for example in maize or cane. In general, farm worker households live in intense and unrelieved poverty, with low nutritional status and few resources to call on when they are retrenched or too sick or old to work.

In terms of land needs, the primary and most strongly articulated demand from presently employed and recently retrenched farm workers across the country is the desire to have a secure place to stay which is not conditional on employment. For many, having a residential plot presumes some space to garden or keep small stock, especially chickens.

There are various viewpoints on where residential rights should be secured. Some farm workers want to remain on the farms where they have grown up, but want full security and rights over a demarcated site. Others want to move off farms, although they have problems with existing urban settlement.

Most farm workers and former farm workers are too poor to acquire residential land from their own resources. The few who have sites have usually obtained them with the help of their employers. Most are living as rent paying tenants. They are acutely aware that they will not be able to secure a residential site without direct, unconditional state assistance.

At the same time, there is some ambivalence about agri-villages. Many workers feel uncomfortable with the idea of socially homogeneous and closed settlements that confine access to farm worker households. They are also concerned about the kinds of control that may be exerted by dominant local farming interests. If these two exigencies are modified, many workers might favour the development of agri-villages, where appropriate.

Many, often older farm workers who still have memories of – although not necessarily connections with – communities in former homelands, were interested in accessing residential land in villages and settlements. Younger farm workers were generally more reluctant to move into former reserves, as were people who had consciously left their villages to get away from family or traditional patronage.

In general, farm worker households live in intense and unrelieved poverty, with low nutritional status and few resources

Both because of low pay and the nature of the work they do, there is also a demand for productive land among farm workers and former farm workers. Those who presently do not have arable rights want them, mostly for gardening, sometimes for field crops. Farm workers who have garden plots and/or keep livestock want to increase their holdings or production capacity. Mostly, they are involved or interested in micro production to supplement their household diet, directly or through sales.

Others – presently employed and former farm workers – are interested in becoming independent small scale surplus producers. This interest is almost exclusively articulated by men, who can envisage themselves as small farmers keeping herds or growing vegetables. Apart from the material support that would have to go into realising this interest, considerable attention would have to be paid to developing farm worker management capacity, which is a gap they realise needs attention.

The position of fully proletarianised farm workers is not much different from that of labour tenants, although labour tenants' attachment to and interest in the land as semi-independent, not necessarily commercial, producers is possibly stronger.

The primary demand from farm workers across the country is for a secure place to stay

able to access full-time jobs on farms other than in domestic service but they make up the overwhelming majority of seasonal and casual workers.

Conditions in the Western Cape vary by the type of produce farmed and the scale of the enterprise. Nevertheless, unlike the rest of the country, which has seen a steady decline in employment, agricultural employment in the Western Cape has continued to increase for more than two decades, growing at eight to nine times the national average from 1980 to 1991/1992 (Wesso 1995).

Social and working conditions for farm workers vary within arable production by crop, scale and intensity of production as well as physical location. They also differ between arable and livestock production, and within livestock by branch: dairy, extensive and intensive, and feedlot production.

Across the country farm workers and their families live in relative degrees of integration with and isolation from each other and other communities. On many farms in most of the provinces, a core workforce lives on the farm with their families. They are joined, where appropriate and for limited periods of time, by casual or seasonal workers who often live in makeshift accommodation.

But there is much variation. On the intensive and highly profitable fruit and wine farms of the Western Cape, for example, most farm workers live on farms in housing complexes constructed by farmers in a tied cottage system which simultaneously stabilises farm worker communities and engenders a form of servitude which undermines their organisation, independence and mobility.

By contrast, more than two thirds of the 2 500 strong workforce on the Skuinsdrif Irrigation Scheme in the Marico District in North West live in surrounding villages in former Bophuthatswana. In the canelands of KwaZulu-Natal and fruit farms of the Western Cape, many farm workers live as migrants in hostels or compounds.

Conditions of employment for workers in commercial agriculture are concentrated in the lowest quintile of the formal sector waged work continuum. They share this ignominious position with workers in domestic service and segments of other primary and service workers.

But their conditions are also differentiated by race, gender and age, as well as by the division between full-time and part-time, seasonal and casual work. Full-time workers receive better rates of pay and earn more consistently than seasonal and casual or part-time workers, who tend to be women – and children – who work at lower rates in periodic bouts of employment.

Labour tenants

> *"Labour tenancy represents an intermediate stage in the transition from cash or crop tenancy to full proletarianisation. Its expansion into the most common form of labour in much of South Africa occurred from the second decade of this century and is inseparable from the land dispossession of the African majority on the one hand, and the capitalisation of agricultural production on the other."* (Marcus 1989)

There is a demand for productive land among farm workers and former farm workers

Labour tenancy – the provision of labour to the land owner in exchange for residential, arable and/or grazing rights – remains widespread in KwaZulu-Natal and Mpumalanga, despite active state intervention to eradicate it between 1960 and 1980, when it was outlawed altogether. In northern KwaZulu-Natal, 1,2 million people operate as labour tenants, and the number in Mpumalanga is estimated as 30 000 to 40 000.

The system was flexible with many variants, enabling it to adapt and persist under considerable adversity (Forsyth 1994; Tloolo 1995), as former peasants tenaciously resisted being pushed into wage labour on commercial farms or off the land altogether.

Labour tenancy remains widespread in KwaZulu-Natal and Mpumalanga

At the same time, these pressures – including restricting labour tenants' access to ever smaller areas of land, limiting the numbers and areas for grazing cattle, placing levies on cattle, fields used, household structure and even numbers of people resident per household, and evictions – forced labour tenants into employment barely distinguishable from those of farm workers.

One distinguishing feature of the system for labour tenants was that their terms of tenancy allowed them to look for work outside commercial agriculture, a right denied farm workers by the provisions of the Masters and Servants Acts and the pass laws (Marcus 1989).

The repeal of these laws and the general vacuum around labour legislation in the commercial sector, which persisted for more than a decade, has made it difficult to distinguish between farm workers and labour tenants in terms of their conditions or the alternatives open to them (Forsyth 1994).

Nevertheless, the traditional exchange of labour for certain land rights continues to be pursued by working people on farms or in areas where it has been an historically established practice. In the Mpumalanga districts of Piet Retief, Wakkerstroom, Ermelo and Southern Carolina, for example, there are an estimated 40 000 labour tenant and farm worker households living on some 4 700 commercial farms (Tloolo 1995). Estimates in KwaZulu-Natal indicate that:

> *"..the number of people living under conditions associated with labour tenancy would be in the region of 200 000."* (Forsyth 1994)

This figure represents a significant decline from the 1970 estimate of 400 000. The decline is visible in the Weenen study area, where former labour farms have largely been denuded of their resident African populations and are now used for year-round or seasonal grazing (Cross *et al* 1995). Most Weenen farmers now pick up labour from the former reserves, informal settlements, transit camps and freehold areas where displaced and local farm workers live.

Given the erosion of labour tenancy, issues arising from the practice only come into focus when tenants are evicted or lose access to land, either because of a change of ownership or of land use.

Conditions vary from community to community, but in general many labour tenants do not derive most of their income from their use of land. The assets they have are concentrated in livestock, although in the recent past livestock seems to have been lost rapidly due to the combined effect of evictions, threat of evictions and drought (Tloolo 1995; Cross *et al* 1995).

Livestock ownership in and between labour tenant communities ranges quite considerably. This is clearly illustrated in the southern Mpumalanga study of six labour tenant communities. Table 5 shows that while in some communities most households had cattle, in most communities the majority of households had none. In addition, there were often significant differences in the number of cattle held by stock owners, with only a few able to keep a herd of any size.

Table 5: Labour tenant cattle holdings in Mpumalanga

Location	Households with cattle	Average number per household	Range
Sulphur Springs (Piet Retief)	21%	8	8
De Magratie (Ermelo)	23%	12	6-16
Hlelo (Piet Retief)	40%	5	–
Iswepe (Piet Retief)	47%	8	3-18
Pampoens-kraal (Piet Retief)	64%	5	3-30
Zaaihoek (Wakkerstroom)	78%	10	2-30

Labour tenants are interested in land and have a rich knowledge and experience of arable production

At the best end of the continuum are communities like Gannahoek in KwaZulu-Natal and Zaaihoek in Mpumalanga.

❒ Gannahoek

Gannahoek is a particularly close and stable labour tenant community which goes back at least 100 years. It is an active farming community, with fairly large cattle and livestock holdings averaging 16 head per household, which are kept for commercial as well as traditional purposes. Most household income is derived from pensions, labour on farms, remittances and stock sales, mostly on their own but sometimes in combination.

When the Gannahoek community bought 578 hectares of their farm with an interest free loan for R210 000, they were able to provide a deposit of R5 200 from their savings – although they now face the difficult, possibly insurmountable task of paying back the loan. There is inequality and poverty in the community, but relatively more people are better off, with only 43% of households reporting periodic food shortages (Forsyth 1994).

Labour tenants rank grazing land third, giving preference to land for cultivation and then gardening

❒ Zaaihoek

The Zaaihoek community in Mpumalanga lives on the land of an absentee farmer, which they have fought to retain despite threats of eviction. They are organised under Chief Mthetwa, who is respected and contributes to the stability of the community.

Zaaihoek is an active farming community which, unlike many other labour tenant communities in surrounding areas, has access to and actively uses land for cultivation. Soils are fairly good and, on average, people plough between one and three hectares. More than half the households (57%) sell produce, generating an average monthly income of R700. This, together with a small amount of livestock sales, constitutes a substantial part of the cash income brought into labour tenant homes.

At the same time, there is a low rate of formal employment in the community: 14%. Most people work as general farm labourers or are employed in forestry as log cutters. The majority earn less than R100 a month, reflecting wage rates that are particularly poor and even compare badly with waged incomes reported by labour tenants in other communities.

Poverty in the community is more widespread than in Gannahoek, with 79% of households reporting periodic food shortages. Yet they remain an active, viable agricultural producing community with strong interests in and knowledge of production on the land where they are settled. They want more land to develop their existing farming capacity, and their land needs remain unsatiated.

❒ Oshishini and Sulphur Springs

More commonly, towards the bottom end of the continuum of labour tenant communities is Oshishini in Muden in KwaZulu-Natal, and Sulphur Springs in Piet Retief in Mpumalanga. In Oshishini, only a minority of the 61 households who make up the settled community were born, raised and worked as labour tenants for the previous farm owner. Most came to the farm after 1978, often from other farms. They invariably work for the owner, albeit with limited rights to run stock.

Most incomes in the community derive from pensions, followed by remittances, then local waged work, including farm work and informal sector activities such as craft and beer sales. Most households have no land under cultivation, largely because of the drought or because they are not allowed to plough. The community does run a herd, principally for consumption and ritual purposes.

While cattle holdings average out to five head of cattle per household, in fact the reported distribution is far more uneven: 21% of households have no cattle while only 12% have between 10 and 20 head, with the remainder holding fewer than nine. Periodic food shortages are endemic for most households, with only about 10% experiencing no shortage at any time in the year (Forsyth 1994).

Forty years ago the labour tenant community at Sulphur Springs enjoyed an abundance of water from streams and springs. The community ploughed large tracts of land, growing potatoes, groundnuts, wheat and vegetables, maize and beans. Over the years their access to plough land and stock has been whittled away such that today only a fifth have cattle and 40% of households have residential land only.

Although most economically active members of the community are employed, they earn low wages averaging R100 to R300 a month. They are mostly unable to supplement their income through productive use of the land because of the deteriorating terms of their tenancy.

The land they access now is very rocky and unyielding, as they have been pushed onto more marginal lands while better soils have been taken over for commercial production. The Sulphur Springs community is very poor. They suffer a high infant mortality rate and 71% of households are food short.

Labour tenants have limited access to land and prescribed rights of usage

❒ Land access

Labour tenants have limited access to land and prescribed rights of usage. What they have they use largely for grazing, although the importance of arable land is hard to assess because of drought, seasonality, the allocation of poor quality land and – possibly more importantly – because of uncertainty and insecurity generated by the climate of threatened and actual evictions which has prevailed for more than a decade. Nevertheless, there is an interest in land and a rich repository of knowledge and experience of arable production.

Farm workers and labour tenants are land hungry. Farm workers want secure residential land, while labour tenants want to live and work on the land

Most farmers impose strict stock controls – in both number and kind – on labour tenant households. The land demand of many labour tenants is therefore related to a desire to increase their cattle and diversify their stock holdings.

In KwaZulu-Natal, for example, labour tenant demand for grazing land is among the highest in the province. This is not surprising given that hardly any other micro, surplus or commercialising producers have stock holdings of any worth. Even then, labour tenants rank grazing land third, giving preference to land for cultivation and then gardening.

In addition to wanting more production land, security of tenure is a foremost concern for labour tenants. As a landed interest group, labour tenants have historically been weakly organised. Many communities have been broken or seriously eroded in the course of eviction. Those who have been able to retain a core of households as present day tenants or former labour tenants, have few resources and very limited institutional capacity.

The prospect of land reform has stimulated populist mobilisation, with threatened mass land invasions if land grievances remain unattended. Several locally negotiated undertakings began prior to the April 1994 elections, but they have only begun to bear fruit in the broader policy frame of the present Government's land reform initiatives.

The moratorium on evictions and the publication of the Land Reform (Labour Tenants) Act for public comment holds some prospect for existing labour tenants in the province. It is unlikely that already evicted labour tenants will benefit much from the redistribution process – although the Act proposes legal recourse to evictions that have taken place since its date of publication. In addition, labour tenants who use the Act to access land will be given priority in the redistribution process.

However, the landed connections of many former labour tenants have been severed for many years. They are likely to respond to reform initiatives designed to bring people back onto the land in much the same way as farm workers and landless rural dwellers resident in former reserves.

Conclusion

Farm workers and labour tenants are land hungry. Farm workers are particularly concerned to secure residential land which is disentangled from their conditions of employment. Labour tenants want security on the land, to live and to work it. They have a strong interest in independent production, an interest which also exists among some male farm workers, although it is weaker and more qualified.

Farm workers want better pay and the removal of discriminatory employment and pay practices which disadvantage women. Establishing wage levels for farm workers that meet and improve household income is an imperative for rural development. In the absence of directed effort in this regard, serious consideration needs to be given to allocating land to, and changing stock holding rights for, farm workers who live on commercial farm land.

Evicted labour tenants currently residing on black owned farms exacerbate land pressures for struggling black micro and surplus producers. The effects of labour tenancy are thus felt at a number of different class levels.

Both farm workers and labour tenants constitute a rich living repository of knowledge and experience in agricultural production. They are also central to stable social development in the countryside, which is why it is important to address their needs and interests in any land and agrarian reform programme.

CHAPTER FIVE

BLACK MICRO, SURPLUS AND COMMERCIAL PRODUCERS

Historically, agricultural production by African producers has been seriously constrained by a system designed expressly to disable and exclude them from engaging in the commercial sector. Coloured and Indian farmers too have been disadvantaged through active and passive discriminatory policies and practices designed to establish and support white commercial production.

People's involvement in growing food and keeping animals can be located on a continuum of production stretching from micro through surplus to commercial producers

Yet in most parts of the country many people still try to involve themselves in agricultural activity. Individual and household involvement in growing food and keeping animals can be located on a continuum of production which stretches from micro through surplus to commercial producers.

While each category reflects differences in the scale, intensity and significance of agriculture for the people involved, none of these groups are static. Not only do they exist in relation to one another, but there is also mobility between them. Under present conditions, most people hover between micro and occasional surplus production, with few being able to sustain regular surplus production or push into full commercial activity.

Micro producers

Agricultural production on a micro scale is largely but not exclusively a rural phenomenon, made possible by the minuscule land access afforded a large proportion of the population through modified traditional tenure systems and through rent, proxy or labour tenancy.

Micro producers are concentrated on traditional, state and black freehold land, while some live in urban settlements, mostly outside major metropolitan centres, and there is some micro production on commercial land by some farm workers.

However, most operate in the former bantustans on communal land, where the endurance of micro producers is intimately linked at an institutional level with traditional authorities, who provide cheap access to land for shelter, resources and agricultural production. In turn, micro producers are often among the staunchest supporters of traditional authorities, particularly in resisting pressures from commercialising producers in their midst to privatise and accumulate land.

Hostel growers

In the urban community of Tshikota outside Louis Trichardt in Northern Province, in addition to some maize cultivation on township plots, some residents and hostel dwellers farm on vacant land around the town.

A small group of hostel dwellers have harnessed the outflow from the hostel drains to establish a small irrigation system. They sell their produce to hawkers in Louis Trichardt. Produce from other plots is either for home consumption or for sale to hawkers and residents in Tshikota on an informal basis (District Report Far North 1995).

Micro production often operates cheek by jowl with surplus, commercialising and established commercial farming. In urban and peri-urban settlements, a growing number of residents are making the most of their ready access to piped water to establish vegetable gardens. This growth in urban micro production reflects the scale of recent settlement by people displaced from the countryside, as much as a need to grow food for own consumption.

The demand for land among micro producers is essentially a survival strategy. For many, micro production represents the difference between hunger and starvation

The demand for land among micro producers is essentially a survival strategy, in conditions where formal sources of income are at best insecure, increasingly absent and where opportunities to diversify sources of income are notably lacking. For many, micro production represents the difference between hunger and starvation.

A large number of rural people have no access to arable land, although the proportion differs in different parts of the countryside across South Africa. In KwaZulu-Natal, for example, in the Weenen-Escourt study area 61% of respondents reported no allocated arable land, whereas in the Mhlatuze catchment study area only 30,5% reported that they had no arable land. In the communal areas of the Eastern Cape, 66% of households had no arable land and only half the households had gardens.

The constraint on micro production is not only land, but also lack of capital, limited water and general insecurity

Between a third and two thirds of those who do have arable land use it, climatic conditions permitting. They mainly grow for consumption, in order to save on purchasing food – the largest single item of household expenditure – or to add some variety to their diets. There is very little surplus which is sold or exchanged.

Land demand by micro producers suggests that they want to continue producing, ideally under less arduous conditions, but not necessarily for commercial purposes.

The available evidence suggests that the constraint on micro production is not only land, but also lack of capital, limited water and general insecurity. In the Ciskei, one of the main reasons why so many fields are left fallow is that, thanks to 'betterment schemes', they are situated away from residential plots and therefore cannot readily be protected from theft and predation. In areas dependent solely on rainfall, it is often not worth investing in cultivation, as costs are high and outputs uncertain.

Moreover, to farm successfully, farmers must commit themselves to stay in one place to work the land. This may conflict with their need to be mobile to take advantage of possible work opportunities.

Like capital and land, labour is unevenly spread across households. That everybody with arable holdings does not cultivate is indicative of structural constraints facing resource poor households.

Micro production presently takes place in conditions of no or low infrastructural provision, particularly the absence of easily accessible water, which aggravates an already serious labour constraint in many rural households.

Food security is a major problem in most households and:

> *"...the fact that their subsistence environment provides such a low level of food security for them is a source of concern....Some of the advantages of land as a free good are*

In Supingstad in North West, nobody had planted since 1992 because of drought, and local chicken flocks were almost entirely wiped out by Newcastle disease in 1994.

lost to marginal households. Interventions which might enable poorer households to use land as a more central component of their coping strategies could make a critical difference.” (Sapsford 1995)

Survey data collected nationally indicates that income from formal employment remains the major source of household income, although everywhere the security of formal employment income has been seriously undercut by rising unemployment.

Other important sources of household income are pensions and then remittances, with independent business trailing at the end. There is very little informal sector activity, with the limited opportunities available concentrated principally in low income retail.

Stockholding is minimal – at best a handful of chickens, a pig or two and perhaps a few goats. More rarely, some people hold one or two cattle. In the Eastern Cape, where livestock production is the dominant branch of farming, for example, about 30% to 40% of communal households have no livestock at all. This proportion rises to between 51% and 68% in the study areas in KwaZulu-Natal.

A few are able to derive a little income occasionally, but mostly they hold animals to meet some of their household consumption needs, and their livestock holdings are too small to satisfy even minimal ceremonial demands required by custom and tradition.

The significance of micro production for poor households should not be underestimated. Although their position is exceedingly precarious, it need not be so. The challenge is to stimulate the independent productive activities of micro producers and strengthen their involvement in agriculture by addressing land and other resource constraints.

> The challenge is to stimulate the productive activities of micro producers by addressing land and other resource constraints

Surplus and commercial producers

In most parts of the country there are pockets of black surplus and commercial producers. Essentially they exist – or have come into being – by way of four routes: as surviving peasantry, through industrial or professional employment, through schemes of previous bantustan governments, or through commercial outgrower schemes.

Coloured Reserve Areas

In Coloured Reserve Areas of Western Cape, agricultural productivity has declined on both marginal and fertile lands through a combination of factors. In addition to uncertainties generated by the previous government's efforts to privatise communal land and thereby remove established usufruct rights, coloured areas have had minimal or no state support and little access to extension and credit facilities.

These problems, combined with negative socio-economic factors – especially low wages and little capital reserve – have reduced Coloured Reserve Areas to seasonal labour pools for adjacent farmers and a refuge for the young, the old and the unemployed. For the most part farming is only practised part-time by pensioners, the disabled and 'weekend farmers'. Generally produce is only cultivated for household consumption (Wesso 1995).

Most commercial and surplus producers whose roots are in the peasantry were born on or near the land they work

❒ The surviving peasantry

The first route is internal to existing black landed relations. Some surplus and commercial producers are rooted in historically established peasant production relations which have survived into the present. The remnants of this peasantry have been contained in pockets on some mission land, on some black freehold land and on some former trust and tribal land, where a combination of factors have allowed more than subsistence production.

Key among the factors determining their survival are that: access to arable land has been average or above average, strict controls have been exercised over human and stock populations levels, resources have not been diverted for company or white commercial use and, in the case of sugar and timber, the nature of the crop has generated a regular cash income for producer households.

Livestock accumulation has been possible where those in positions of power and authority have selectively turned a blind eye to stock limitation regulations – often for select individuals – and/or where individuals have spread their stock holdings across various tenure systems.

For the most part, commercial and surplus producers whose roots are in the peasantry were born on or near the land they work. However, there are also many instances of historical peasant communities which have survived despite suffering forced removal, as the case of the community at Batloung ba ga Shole in North West province sharply highlights.

❐ The employment route

A second route into surplus and/or commercial agricultural production is through industrial or professional employment, capital accumulation through business ventures and then investment in farming.

Since remittances from formal sector employment are particularly important to the success of all black small scale agriculture, the difference between this route and that of the historical peasantry lies more in whether the land base existed in the first instance or not. The feature of this second path – which is more the exception than the rule – is that the land base does not exist. Rather, it is acquired.

The practical experience of entry into commercial agriculture through resources secured in business or professional or industrial employment is well illustrated by examples from Thaba Nchu in the Free State, where it was still possible to acquire African privately owned land for farming.

Historically and at present, the experience of private ownership of land has had mixed outcomes. For many African farmers, purchase of privately owned land has not been a point of departure for successful farming.

Whether in Thaba Nchu in the Free State, or Valdezia in Northern Province or Ramatlabama in North West, privately held land is under used and undeveloped. Where it is rented out, some black people have been given access to farm land which they would not have had. But this land has often been let to white commercial farmers, which is inimical to wider distribution of land.

For many African farmers, purchase of privately owned land has not been a point of departure for successful farming

What private land ownership has done, in fact, is provide some black land owners with financial liquidity. While it has ultimately led to the dispossession of some, for others it has led to expanded opportunities for education and employment for landowners' children, which over generations has transformed many into professionals with little interest in agriculture.

❐ The former reserves

A third route into possible surplus or commercial production was through the governments of the former reserves.

This happened in one of two ways. The first way was via development projects created by the reserves' various parastatals to stimulate small scale commercial production.

Invariably, these projects have been centrally managed, capital intensive schemes which have neither enabled independent small scale commercial production nor had any significant impact on job creation and broader rural development in the areas where they are located. Many of the schemes are running at a loss and have become heavy financial burdens on provincial governments.

> Development projects in former reserves have neither enabled independent small scale commercial production nor had any significant impact on development

A peasant community in Vryheid

The community living on land owned by the Evangelical Lutheran Church of South Africa at its Bethal farm near Vryheid in KwaZulu-Natal is an example of an historical peasant community which still actively works the land.

Surrounded by white, privately owned land, the farm covers 2 108 hectares, just under half of which the Church farms commercially using white management.

The 63 households living on the 'community' section of the holding use 45 hectares for residential purposes, 124 hectares for cultivation and some of 929 hectares of veld for grazing. On average, arable land access per household is two hectares.

Almost all households (86%) plant their arable allocations, mostly to maize although there is also limited vegetable production. Most use bought fertilisers and employ hired labour. A large proportion of households (64%) have some cattle, with just over a quarter owning 10 head or more. The only other animals they have are chickens.

Restrictions informed by 'betterment' and other state policies have been externally imposed by the Church on the community. They have had a negative impact, acting as a major constraint on more diversified crop production as well as livestock holdings.

The Bethal community wants more land to plough but past efforts to secure it have failed. They are also constrained by cash, which impedes their farming activities. Among other grievances they have is that they are expected to hire the mission tractor, which they feel is unnecessary as it is also partly theirs since they are the mission. The farm manager of the commercial section refuses to plough their fields (Marcus 1995).

The Ramatlabama community

The 70 households of the Batloung ba ga Shole community bought the farm Putfontein on December 12, 1886. They lived there until 1977, when they were removed to Ramatlabama, north of Mafikeng, where most of them now live. The move saw their land holdings reduced from seven to 15 morgen arable plots plus access to communal grazing land, to eight morgen for both cultivation and stock.

Nineteen farmers at Putfontein had bought land privately from white farmers and registered it in their own names. They had mineral rights to the land and they worked the 50 to 100 morgen farms in much the same way as the rest of the Putfontein households.

When they were removed they were promised farms double the size of the ones they owned because they were losing mineral rights, but they ended up getting about 45 hectares – less land than they originally had. Few owners work their land, and many have entered into share cropping arrangements with neighbouring land hungry micro and surplus producers.

In addition, there are 18 farmers on what is known as the Sekai block. The Sekai land was bought by the South African Development Trust and incorporated into former Bophuthatswana. It was divided into 22 farms – each approximately 300 hectares, with a house, water pump, reservoir and farm shed – which were leased for seven years to the farmers with an option to buy.

The land was bought as extensive arable land, despite rainfall and other conditions making it unsuitable for cultivated crop land, because the farmers who had sold it had rapidly brought it under the plough to take advantage of the premium offered by the state for cultivated land. The current owners reverted back to extensive grazing land.

Although their leases have been extended, the farmers are concerned about their future on the land. They want to buy their farms. They also want to extend their holdings, but are aware that there are people with less land who are in greater need than themselves.

They make a living on what they have, although reversion to grazing means that the viability of their farms will depend on them expanding to two to 10 times the current size, depending on whether they rely on planted or natural pasturage.

> Land allocations are too small, and 'farmers' have little or no say over production procedures and financial management

Everywhere, their land allocations are too small and production equipment is usually centrally owned and controlled. 'Farmers' have little or no say over production procedures and financial management, and often there are stringent regulations about the presence of the farmers on the scheme and the uses to which they put their land.

Struggling small farmers

Researchers interviewed a self-made businessman who has become a successful farmer. He was formerly a teacher who had no land, but was able to invest some of his earnings as well as profits from an inherited small business into local land purchase and commercial production.

He worked his farms and expanded his retail business interests over the years to become one of the most successful businessmen in Thaba Nchu. In October 1994, he employed six full-time workers on his three farms. He had 132 cattle on his two southern farms and extensive plough lands. On his northern farm he had reduced his field crops to animal fodder.

By March 1995, he had cut his workforce to four. He no longer cultivated the arable portions of his southern farms because the combined effects of drought and rising costs made it unprofitable. He was thinking of getting out of agriculture, because of personal health reasons and because his six children – all highly educated – were unlikely to take over farming from him.

On a 300 morgen farm privately owned by four Africans in the south of Thaba Nchu, one of the owners rents his 100 morgen section to a tenant.

The tenant grew up in one of the Thaba Nchu locations and spent 19 years as a migrant worker in Bloemfontein, employed by South African Railways. In 1982 he gave up his job and started selling coal and sand for plastering. He rented the farm he is now working in 1983 and started farming.

In October 1994 he had 20 cattle and 16 sheep on the land. He employed one man for R90 a month and a 12,5 kilogram bag of mealie meal, and a youth for R60 a month to supervise the livestock. He also kept pigs (Murray (ed) 1995).

Although parastatal schemes have let a few individuals into commercial production, they have done so in a narrowly defined and disempowering way

While each project differs in detail, the position of the black commercial farmers of the Bosele Cooperative in the Taung Irrigation Scheme in North West is typical.

Although these schemes have let a few selected individuals into commercial production, they have done so in a narrowly defined and invariably disempowering way. On the 'pineapple kibbutzes' created in the early 1980s in former Transkei, for instance, the farmers 'managed' while the parastatal hired labour to grow and pick the pineapples.

For many participants, these schemes have frustrated rather than stimulated their capacity and interest in farming. Few have flourished and many have gone into further decline in the face of policy uncertainty, state reorganisation and reviews of state spending.

Thus, when the state began to reduce its support services to the Keiskammahoek small scale dairy farmer scheme in the former Ciskei, for instance, only a handful of individuals were able to use the opportunity to diversify their farming operations. Most stuck with dairy, although production declined, demanding a new injection of state finance and services support (Van Averbeke 1995).

A second opening created for surplus and commercial production by the state began in the early 1980s with the lease or sale of farms acquired by the former reserves through 'homeland consolidation'. Many of these farms have gone to politicians, chiefs, senior civil servants, police and businessmen. There is a high rate of absenteeism – 75% in former Transkei. Payments are often not made and land is frequently left unused.

❒ Outgrower schemes

The fourth route into surplus and commercial agricultural production is through corporate outgrower schemes. This is a more recent development which is driven by specific sectors of agribusiness – forestry and sugar in particular.

The models that have been developed have been significantly influenced by the existing tenure systems and patriarchal relations of the former reserves of Mpumalanga and KwaZulu-Natal, as well as the particular institutional style of the respective corporations. The focus here is on the experiences of KwaZulu-Natal, aspects of which apply in Mpumalanga.

> Corporate outgrower schemes have been influenced by the existing tenure systems and patriarchal relations of the former reserves of Mpumalanga and KwaZulu-Natal

Developed in the first instance by the sugar industry, the model in KwaZulu-Natal is not centred around the classic small farmer development path, where farmers own their land and can develop it as they wish. Rather, it is built around contract farming, an institutional innovation where:

Irrigation projects in former Ciskei

Six existing medium size irrigation projects in Ciskei cover 2 768 hectares and involve 2 306 rural households. Nine percent – 214 households – are small commercial producers on four to 12 hectares, while 91% or 2 092 households are micro producers growing food on plots which range in size from 0,1 to 0,25 hectares (Van Averbeke 1995)

The Taung Irrigation Scheme

The Taung and Vaalharts irrigation schemes form a single functional unit even though they are divided by a provincial boundary between North West and the Northern Cape. Farmers on both schemes grow the same crops – lucerne, peanuts, maize, cotton and beans – but operate under very different conditions.

The Taung scheme's farmers have been allocated 10 hectares each, which they rent from the scheme. Farmers share the use of irrigation equipment – four farmers per pivot – and one tractor, all of which belong to the scheme.

Crops are harvested by contractors and there is no processing on the scheme as there are no facilities. Farmers have to rely on casual workers, who they pay R5 to R6 a day, and they feel they have little hope of hiring permanent labour.

They want to expand their holdings into viable units of around 40 hectares, and they want to buy the land they farm. They feel the pivots have been paid for several times over: each farmer has paid R6 000 every six months for the last 13 years, which adds up to an outlandish R624 000 per pivot.

By contrast, on the Vaalharts scheme, white farmers farm on plots ranging from 25 to 190 hectares, and farmers with plots of less than 50 hectares tend to rent additional pastoral land.

They own their land and equipment and employ between 10 and 22 full-time workers. They also employ seasonal labour for planting, weeding and harvesting at between R8 and R10 a day. The number of seasonal workers varies from five to 120 per farm.

The relationship between agribusiness and outgrowers is conditioned by the contract

> *"...the company delegates some or all of the responsibility for production, but retains control of processing and marketing."* (MacDonald and Vaughan 1995)

The relationship between agribusiness and the farmers is conditioned by the contract.

> *"The essence of the contract is the same everywhere: the miller advances credit to the grower and takes as collateral the future crop. In return for an assured throughput of cane for the mill, the mill owners provide finance, extension services and, at present, a guaranteed market for the grower."* (Draper 1994)

Other forms of security are not needed because of the high value added during the processing phase. The contract encapsulates a very uneven power relation and is a source of considerable tension for producers. Producers say over production varies and is conditioned by a number of factors. Company style is one. While some mills assume almost total responsibility for production, others leave producers with some space for initiative, for example in the Tongaat-Hulett north area of KwaZulu-Natal.

Local contract capacity is another tension. The assumption of the model is that field preparation services, harvesting and transporting of cane to the mill, for example, will be done by local people providing contracting services. The experience is that local contractors face major constraints. Like producers, they are subject to labour constraints in high migrancy areas.

And then they have to weigh up the opportunity costs of taking on the onerous regime associated with contracting services when there are potentially less arduous and more lucrative alternatives (Vaughan 1993). The plethora of small grower contractors spawned by the cane schemes, in fact, reflects an unmet land demand. If they could, many contractors would prefer to concentrate on growing rather than servicing growers.

A third tension is the form in which credit is offered. In both timber and cane it is offered in kind, against the completion of specified tasks, and is automatically deducted at the end of the production cycle from the value of the crop.

In the case of timber the loan amounts to about 15% of the final amount, in sugar it equals about 25% of the total value of the crop. The approach to credit allocation and loan retrieval practices thus constitutes a substantial intervention by agribusiness in the management of producer farm budgets.

There is tension in the form in which credit is offered, and in local contract capacity

Farming commonage in Vleifontein

In the remote rural town of Vleifontein in Northern Province, a group of residents enthusiastically farm the municipal commonage under difficult conditions. They lack land, security, water, tractors and services, and they face encroachment from wild animals and stray cattle. They actively use the land they access and are in need of more.

Meanwhile, over the fence, land which civil servants of the former Venda gave themselves, lies idle. The farmers from Vleifontein want to use this land for farming, but the people they are negotiating with about accessing it are the people who own it (Northern Transvaal Land Research Group 1995).

Small growers face other problems. Cane production does boost household income, but it does not take cane growing households out of poverty. In the Umvoti Valley (Institute for Social and Economic Research 1994)), for example, income from cane growing contributed 19% to total household income for dryland producing households, which was approximately three times more than the average contribution of agriculture to black household income in the former reserves, but which did not push their total average income above the primary household subsistence level.

Many cane growers combine the labour of family members with hired wage labour, but struggle to pay competitive wages

For growers using irrigation, cane production's contribution to total household income rose significantly to 47%, pushing average total household income above the household subsistence level but not out of relative poverty.

The average cane plot is 2,5 hectares, which is little different from the arable holdings of micro and commercialising producers in the former reserves, but which is estimated to be four (for irrigated) to 13 (for rainfed) times too small for viable commercial cane production (Sokhela in Draper 1994).

Contract cane growers also face problems of inefficiency and bad timing. A common complaint is that fertilisers are delivered far too late to be of maximum benefit.

In the case of timber, some woodlots in the Ndundulu area which have been absorbed into Mondi's Khulunathi project were not well surveyed and supported, and the trees are not maturing properly. Moreover, the project, which covers nine areas of northern KwaZulu, has concentrated on using more accessible land with favourable soil types. The effect has been to reduce the amount of land available to food production – and more significantly, the crop depletes the amount of water available for cultivation, grazing and other purposes.

Many cane growers combine the labour of family members with hired wage labour. However, they offer very limited and insecure wage earning opportunities and are themselves severely labour constrained because they have to compete for labour with better placed employers (white commercial farmers, for example) and/or more lucrative employment opportunities (urban and industrial).

Growers are disgruntled about the quality and quantity of work done by the people they hire, which is intensified by the cash flow problems which arise from employing labour in conditions where finance is forthcoming only after the work is completed.

Contract producers are mono-crop and mono-corporate dependent. This kind of production boosts household income and the contribution of agriculture to it. However, up until now, it has inhibited the ability of households to diversify income sources.

There is evidence of positive correlations between multiple sources of income and well being, and between cash income and capacity to produce and diversify.

Turning to land demand, there is an expressed wish for land among producers working crops supported by agribusiness, although it is not entirely unambiguous and differs by crop, as the case study of timber and sugar in KwaZulu-Natal clearly shows.

Where institutional and infrastructural supports are in place, interest in land for sugar is clear, and it is stronger than interest in timber because the returns on capital investment and labour are evident in the short term.

More generally, however, given the same or a similar regime of supports and services, land demand would be more strongly directed to an interest in alternative crops and/or crop diversification. The challenge would be to attract other segments of

Mono-crop and mono-corporate dependence has boosted household income but has inhibited the ability of households to diversify income sources

Timber outgrower problems

"You can be a timber grower, but you can't eat those trees. You have to be a member of the community garden so that for the time your trees are still growing, at least you have something to hold onto. That is why we encourage one another to participate in both timber growing and food crops." (Timber Grower, Ndundulu)

Timber is harvested every eight years. A grower needs three harvestable hectares per annum if timber is to be the major source of household income. In a seven year rotation period a timber grower would need at least 21 hectares. In the Ndundulu area, the average timber grower has two hectares.

As they are presently set up, small grower timber schemes do not provide greater food security for rural households. The income from timber is too small and too infrequent to meet regular food needs (MacDonald and Vaughan 1995).

Vegetable production

Small scale vegetable production could become a more important activity than it presently is for micro and surplus producers. But current opportunities offered by gardening are limited and vegetable production tends to be a marginal activity for households who have alternatives.

Where garden plots and cane exist together, as on the Biyela Irrigation Scheme in KwaZulu-Natal, for example, people deploy labour on the cane fields before they work their gardens. And where household labour is limited they tend to choose to work the cane rather than the plots. Nevertheless, it is important to create and support such opportunities because, even if gardens are under utilised, they are a vital resource for poor households.

The demand for freehold tenure is fairly strongly articulated by commercialising producers. It reflects the dominant influence of private property

agro-industry – banana, fruit or avocado producers, for example – into a process which the state could not begin to resource on its own.

The demand for freehold tenure is fairly strongly articulated by commercialising producers. It reflects the dominant influence of private property on social, economic and especially financial relations. But it also indicates other tensions.

There is tension between tenure systems which accord rights differently: communal tenure constrains private accumulation of property and investment, and does not necessarily guarantee individual tenure security at an expanded level. And there is tension between contract and corporate producers, where contract growers are constrained in their choice of crop and their ability to access financial and other services outside those offered by agribusiness for specific crops.

In sum, land demand in outgrower schemes is significantly influenced by the kinds of corporate intervention, the responses of traditional authorities, the nature of the crop and conditions of its production, and the provision of water and infrastructure (Vaughan and MacDonald 1995).

Contract farming generates an elite in a very flat pyramid. Whether it is in fact a path of development which will allow commercialising producers to 'emerge' – that is to establish themselves as commercial producers – depends on changes internal and external to the present system.

Household incomes

In the pilot land reform area of KwaZulu-Natal, for example, monthly household income for the better off is between R800 and R1 200 and for the elite it is R2 000 or more. Surplus producers grew more than half the maize produced and owned more than half the livestock. On average they had two to three regular formal sector wage incomes per household.

Possibly of more importance is what contract farming does do for micro and surplus producers. Especially in the case of small grower cane, these schemes provide depth and substance to agricultural production for households which otherwise would be far worse off.

Outgrower production remains a real option for a specific type of crop production, particularly timber and cane. It is not a universal panacea, even in KwaZulu-Natal where cane and timber predominate in field crops.

Conclusion

Notwithstanding the interests and concerns that are generated by each particular route into agriculture, surplus and commercial producers have generally similar characteristics and preoccupations.

Surplus petty commodity and commercial producers make up part of the 10% to 15% of better off and elite rural households. They tend

Farming against the odds

In Manenzhe in Northern Province, there is a farmer who grows tomatoes on one hectare of his 10 hectare farm, which he rents for R100 a year. He irrigates the tomatoes from his own borehole but does not have the capital to expand the irrigation to the rest of the land or introduce a more environmentally appropriate irrigation scheme – drip irrigation – which he has unsuccessfully tried to improvise.

He has sold his produce to the Messina and Makhado canning factories in the past, but reported incidents of crops being left to rot while waiting to be graded. His crop has also rotted while waiting for promised transport. As a result of these experiences he has tended not to plant as much recently as he did in the past or is capable of growing (Northern Transvaal Land Research Group 1995).

Surplus and commercial producers have generally similar characteristics and preoccupations to grow more and own more livestock, producing most of the crop and holding most of the herd in any one community. They invariably have more wage earners per household, more sources of income and more cash income.

Surplus commodity and small scale producers often access land but are unable to use it effectively because of production constraints, among them finance and limited water supplies

Those who are producing are interested in getting more land and in increasing arable production. Interest in expanding livestock production is somewhat less strong, regional differences notwithstanding. For the most part, the amount of land wanted by surplus and commercialising producers is modest and takes into account the use they are presently making of land as well as non-land constraints.

Frequently, people said they wanted an addition of about the same as what they are presently working – which for the most part is between two and five hectares. However, the viability of small scale producers working on state or private schemes is often undermined by the scale of their land access. These producers want enough land for commercial viability: often three or four times what they are presently working.

Transport costs for small scale timber producers are estimated to be 280% to 550% higher than for large scale timber growers (Saville 1994).

There is also a strong demand for freehold title, especially for arable production. However, stockholders are more ambivalent. Most want more grazing land but this is not necessarily linked to acquiring freehold title over it.

There are surplus commodity and small scale commercial producers who are not interested in acquiring more land under present conditions. They often access land but are unable to use it effectively because of a number of production constraints, key among them finance and limited or inaccessible water supplies.

Typically, surplus and commercial producers are often able to procure inputs, use machinery and/or hire labour. But often they are disadvantaged by the limited scale and poor terms on which they access inputs and labour.

The impact of these limitations is felt by surplus and commercial producers in the first instance, but they also have knock-on effects up and down stream of surplus and small scale production. Their ability to provide employment opportunities is hampered, conditions of employment are frequently worse but invariably as bad as the lowest in surrounding established commercial agriculture, and they are unable to stimulate the market in supplies and services.

When bio-climatic conditions are favourable, small producers are constrained by a negative marketing environment – especially the narrow crop range and absence of local market places. The high costs and limited nature of transport to markets, especially, has severe adverse effects on their viability.

Many black surplus and commercialising producers face the problem of local patronage networks and graft by processing plant foremen and officials. This not only affects their access to land, but also to transport and marketing outlets.

There is an apparent general willingness among surplus and commercial producers to relocate to improve their access to land and services. However, for most the willingness is based on an implicit assumption that they would retain what they already have and would not forfeit their existing social network. In other words, for many the reason to move would be to expand and access more – not necessarily agricultural – resources and better services.

In summary, surplus commodity and commercial producers need more land, but they also need redress to labour, capital, supports and services – constraints which operate, invariably in combination, to inhibit and contain their potential to flourish.

For many, production is based on meeting consumption needs with intermittent forays into the marketing of surpluses – the frequency of which is largely determined by the relative favourability of climatic and social conditions. But even among those whose foundation is surplus commercial production, many presently hover precariously on the edge of subsistence production because of the constraints they suffer.

CHAPTER SIX

WHITE FARMERS AND CORPORATE AGRICULTURE

White commercial farmers and corporate sector agriculture or 'agribusiness' are established producers with considerable vested interest in the way landed relations are presently organised. They have a keen, albeit somewhat different interest in land reform.

> The experiences of established farmers could help inform new entrants into the commercial sector

Numerically, the largest proportion of commercial producers are family farmers (Marcus and Levin 1994; Beinart 1994). Their experiences of entering farming, setting up, running and developing their enterprises are instructive, and could help inform new entrants to commercial farming. Most farmers come from households with a history and a continued attachment to the land. More rarely, some commercial farmers have come into the sector cold – without roots or training in agriculture.

But none have come without resources. Inheritance and bank credit have served as conduits for keeping successive generations of white farmers on the land.

Developing farms into profitable concerns, however, has also depended on a range of other conditions. Specialisation has been particularly important. The shift from mixed farming to cane, timber and cattle in Melmoth in KwaZulu-Natal in the 1960s, for example, enabled farmers striving to become commercially viable to develop. They were able to adopt:

> *"...strategies to maximise their relative strengths in terms of soil types, micro weather conditions, size of land holdings, labour resources and marketing opportunities."* (Vawda 1994)

Moreover, the establishment and success of commercial farmers was not achieved quickly. In Nkwaleni, where irrigated agriculture is the foundation of farming enterprises, it took several farmers more than the five years stipulated by the government lease scheme to establish themselves. Under the rain-fed conditions of Melmoth, establishing successful farming enterprises took most farmers at least a generation or more, underscoring the importance of the continuity of investment.

Farming in Aberdeen

Under present conditions in Aberdeen, in the Karoo in the Eastern Cape – where an economic unit is considered to be between 8 000 and 9 000 hectares with a carrying capacity of 2 200 small stock units – farmers need a return on capital of between 5% and 6% per annum to survive.

With meticulous planning, enough capital to stock quickly, substantial appropriate guidance and support, and in the absence of drought in an area where drought is endemic, a new farmer will only show a profit after 18 months, all things being equal. Since all things are rarely equal, this scenario is more ideal than actual (Eastern Cape Karoo Study 1995).

A further condition of established commercial agriculture has been relatively abundant cheap labour drawn from the pools of unemployed and under employed households resident on farms, in rural towns and on former reserves which neighbour commercial farmland.

Demand for land among commercial farmers is mixed. While there is evidence of demand for land – especially among cash rich farmers (Beinart 1994) – there are also indications that many commercial farmers have little effective demand.

A lot have expanded, consolidated and intensified production on their enterprises over the past three decades and more. Others, who might have thought of expanding their landholdings, are reluctant or unable to do so for a range of reasons.

Specialisation, capital, planning and cheap labour have been necessary for many commercial farmers to succeed

Farmers often mentioned uncertainties about land and labour reforms. While these concerns affect their confidence, many are ill

Land inequalities

Management of Karoo rangeland requires extensive holdings. However, there are individual and/or family holdings which run to tens of thousands of hectares. Justification of this scale of holdings is dubious in a land hungry situation (Eastern Cape Karoo Study 1995)

informed about government policy and have misapprehensions based largely on rumour and hearsay. Moreover, more often than not, there are other important material considerations which influence whether they increase their landholdings or not.

There is some demand for land among commercial farmers, but many have little effective demand

Limiting factors to commercial expansion

White commercial farmers on the Vaalharts Irrigation Scheme in the Northern Cape, listed the following as limiting factors to expansion:

- Unstable water supply
- Uncertainty about government policy, especially with regard to tax
- Insufficient production related research
- Unstable profit margins
- Lack of capital
- An uncertain economic future
- Labour problems

(Setplan, Northern Cape 1995)

The disabling effects of theft and insecurity in various parts of the countryside, especially those close to large settlements, have been indicated elsewhere.

On these frontiers farmers are either being forced to retreat – 'farming backwards at a hell of a speed', was how one Free State farmer described it – or they are farming under state of emergency conditions with high electric fencing, 24 hour armed patrols and inevitable stock, infrastructure and crop losses.

Where conditions are more secure, commercial farmers are influenced by their knowledge of available land in the context of an active land market. Farms that tend to come onto the market are cither not commercially efficient, not fully developed or in need of a great deal of attention.

In the harsh conditions of the Karoo, where sheep and angora goats are farmed, the view is that buying land is not the issue: buying improvement is. When farms have been developed, they are very costly. For example, on high cost intensive irrigation farms in the Nkwaleni valley of KwaZulu-Natal, purchase prices start at about R3 million. This is an indication of the cost associated with small pieces of developed high value land.

The Wild West

Gert Ferreira holds the western frontier of Botshabelo with guns and dogs and sheer stubbornness around the clock, without which all his livestock would be cleaned out immediately.

He rented his 500 morgen farm for R8 000 a year, and retained it on an indefinite lease from the state on the understanding that he provide a buffer between the people of the sprawling slum settlement and the springbok in the nearby provincial park (Murray (ed) Appendix 5).

Farmers in need of more land often choose to rent, which frequently is less costly in the short to medium term and also more flexible. For many, the most promising alternative – although it is often environmentally unfriendly – is to approach enhanced profitability through specialisation and expansion into retail and manufacturing, a route illustrated by a Levuvhu farmer who set up both nut and fruit processing plants on his land.

Vertical expansion is not an option open to everybody for a number of reasons, which leaves farmers with little choice.

Farming – the bottomless pit

A Northern Province family bought their 18 hectare farm in 1988. It was derelict, comprising an old house without electricity and a crop of mango trees overgrown with vines. They put a lot of money into the farm. They rebuilt the house and planted about 1 000 mango trees.

Seven years down the line they have about 1 250 mango trees – their main cash crop – a number of macadamia trees which are not yet producing and some avocado, litchi and banana trees, mainly for home consumption.

They bought their farm with a loan:

"...and that's your first downfall because you need at least seven years of good rains to pay off the loan. The farm is like a bottomless pit that you have to keep on pouring money into. Often you get nothing back in return."

Although farming contributes to their livelihood they cannot live on farming alone. They feel it is too unstable and not profitable enough. They are not using their farm optimally, irrigating only about a third of their trees from the borehole they had to sink (Northern Province Land Research Group 1995).

Land and labour reforms, theft and insecurity, and lack of water and capital are limitng commercial expansion

Marketing options – comparative choices

When it comes to marketing mangoes, farmers have three choices. They can send the green ones to an achar factory, the very ripe to a juice factory and the semi-ripe to a fruit market in Gauteng.

The last option takes more labour and time because the fruit has to be sorted and packed, and transport has to be organised. Because there are more middle men involved the price has to be good to make it worthwhile. If the market is bad, the farmers save their mangoes for juice (White farmer, Levuvhe).

For commercial farmers the purpose of land reform is to build a class of black farming entrepreneurs

They either have to work more land, or they have to work their land more intensively or, alternatively, they have to switch their farming operations to more profitable segments of the market – the most common trend at present being from field crops to beef and mutton and in stock farming from cattle to game.

The Campbell Conundrum

All the white farmers in Campbell want to expand their farming operations by acquiring more land, but there is very little available on the market. Few farms are sold, and when they are they are bought by local residents.

None of the farmers are prepared to consider the option of vertical expansion, for example opening a butchery, because they lack trained labour and feel that the enterprise would take up too much management time, which would impact negatively on their primary enterprise (Setplan, Northern Cape).

Farmer perceptions of land reform

When it comes to land reform, established commercial farmers have a vision of change which essentially reflects little more than aspects of their common experience, and which displays a parochialism no different from other land interested groups.

They acknowledge that there is a demand and need for land, but immediately erect the inviolability of the *status quo* – particularly with regard to commercially used land – and the limited possibility that it offers for redistributive reform and poverty alleviation. This leads them to pose land issues in a very specific but narrow way which places little emphasis on what people want or the possibilities that might exist or could be created to help them work the land. As one white farmer put it:

> *"Providing the rural poor with land will simply expand the lowest end of the bushveld timeshare market."*

For established commercial farmers the purpose of land reform is more to build a class of black farming entrepreneurs, not unlike themselves, through the operation of a regulated 'classic liberal' market, although many recognise the difficulties of this route.

Many commercial farmers believe that reform has to be directed almost exclusively at state held land and the communal land tenure system.

Some farmers are also open to under utilised, privately held land being drawn into the reform process, but for the most part they believe land 'reform' (transfer) in the private sector must be 'managed by the market'. Land would be acquired by individuals through state guaranteed bank loans, divided up into viable units and accessed conditionally, subject to a farmer proving himself capable of profitable farming.

The necessary support services to assist new farmers – extension, training in financial management, planning etc – would be provided by the state and organised commercial agriculture. Few farmers, however, have given much thought to the implications this would carry for the services they provide. Indeed, there is an assumption that nothing much will change except the volume of outreach.

White farmers are keen to incorporate black commercial farmers, seeing them as a way of securing their own future

With regard to scale, the general feeling of established commercial farmers is that new entrepreneurs would produce on a scale of at least a small commercial holding: that is, the new farmers are envisaged neither as small growers nor as micro producers. Farmers feel the latter are not only likely to fail to deliver food security but might even undermine it.

Commercial farmers feel ambiguous about traditional authority structures. They recognise traditional structures are central to securing many people's access to land, that they maintain some degree of order, and that for many they are an important part of procuring and guaranteeing farmers' labour supply under present conditions.

At the same time traditional structures are an anachronism which would hamper the entrepreneurial farming activities which established farmers see as the way forward. White commercial farmers are also concerned that if land is released from commercial areas it will rapidly be subject to the same pressures operating inside the former reserves or on black freehold land, with the result that land will be used essentially for residential and subsistence purposes.

Commercial farmers fear land reform that does not take into account the need to retain the viability of commercial agriculture

Institutionally, white commercial farmers are well organised through farmers' associations and unions. They are keen to incorporate black commercial farmers, seeing them as a way of securing their own future. They envisage that new black farmers would fit into the current district farmers' and sectoral associations, to learn and to take advantage of the services and protection of an organised body.

Some farmers are more ambiguous, however, over whether their local associations would be open to new black farmers or whether black farmers would have to form their own associations (Marcus and Levin 1993). And unsurprisingly, after years of exclusion and conscious of white farmer ambivalence, black farmers' organisations such as the National African Farmers Union, are wary of incorporation.

Commercial farmers fear land reform that does not take into account the need to retain the viability of commercial agriculture. They envisage their engagement in reform as largely supervisory: to mentor and manage the transition of 'new' black farmers into 'their' world, although presently the farmers who actually practice what they profess in this regard are the exception rather than the rule.

The corporate sector

The corporate sector is interested both in land and land reform. In field crop production, corporate interests dominate cane and timber in Mpumalanga and KwaZulu-Natal.

Timber companies are especially interested in expanding, either by acquiring existing commercial land or through community outgrower schemes in traditional authority areas. Mondi, for example, has made major land purchases in the Eastern Cape.

The sugar industry is interested in continuing to open up new land, although over the past five years the area under cane in

KwaZulu-Natal, for example, has remained fairly constant. Tongaat-Hulett has led the way in accessing land in traditional authority areas for sugar through small grower schemes which it initiated in the early 1970s.

The corporate sector has a direct interest in and vision of land reform which is driven and conditioned, in the first instance, by business needs. The focus is on establishing and developing commercialising producers in order to secure their products for the future. Both their product and economic dominance enables them to adopt a more open and proactive approach, although even then there are important differences between different corporations.

For example, Tongaat-Hulett's initiatives in accessing non-freehold land is a model which has been applied to timber, albeit on a much smaller scale, by Sappi and Mondi over the past decade.

Illovo (CG Smith), by contrast, has been far slower and less proactive in engaging with the model or reform in general, while HL&H is not interested in outgrower schemes at all, preferring to continue operating in white owned commercial farming areas.

Most recently, corporate reform has begun to focus on the transfer of some of its own land holdings to African growers. The Illovo initiative to pilot dedicated land transfers to some 20 medium sized black growers on 90 hectare (initially 35 hectare) land parcels – a total of 1 600 hectares – was worked into its plans to dispose of some 16 000 hectares.

Tongaat-Hulett's pilot land transfer scheme is initially directed towards its own employees and involves leasing and then selling four farms ranging in size from 70 hectares to 117 hectares to establish medium scale growers.

> The corporate sector's interest in and vision of land reform is driven by business needs

In both instances, the positive response from potential producers has been matched by a negative and disabling response from financial institutions. At Illovo, for example, of 120 applicants only 10 were able to mobilise the deposit and not necessarily all of them will be able to sustain repayments on an R80 000 debt without specifically developed supports.

In limiting and directing the scheme to its own employees first, Tongaat-Hulett is looking to their experience, knowledge and interest as selection criteria, not whether they are rich enough to afford the purchase.

Unless finance can be arranged in packages which meet the objectives of these schemes, they will only be able to transfer land horizontally or upwards to the elite – which does not support policy preferences aimed at the very poor and may well nullify other selection criteria, especially experience in producing cane.

> There is a willingness in the corporate sector to engage with the national land reform initiative

There are also initiatives to transfer land for residential and other non-agricultural purposes. Illovo is prepared to earmark some of its non-cane land for sale to community trusts. Mondi and HL&H are looking to transfer land to people they have 'inherited' on farms they have acquired.

Their focus is particularly on housing development along the lines of agri-village models. Their aim is to settle people's residential land needs and ensure production security by controlling who settles on land adjacent to or on their farms and by establishing a labour pool (Fleming 1995).

In general, there is a willingness in the corporate sector to engage actively and proactively with the national land reform initiative. This engagement is hampered by both the novelty of the process – everything is not in place – and lack of a general vision.

CHAPTER SEVEN

TRADITIONAL AUTHORITIES

The Land Reform Research Programme was conducted at a time when there was great uncertainty and lack of clarity on local government issues. However, the research still found that most people who supported the traditional authority system did not necessarily support individual traditional authorities. This chapter contributes to an unresolved and complex debate on the role of traditional authorities in relation to land.

Land allocation is critical to traditional leaders because it is one of the few remaining actual powers they have

Traditional authorities are both a source of land demand and an institutional arrangement which is central to the administration and servicing of land reform in all provinces except Gauteng and the Western Cape. The land allocation function is critical to traditional leaders because it is one of the few remaining actual powers and sources of influence that they have. In KwaZulu-Natal, for example:

> *"...the positions now being taken by the Amakhosi on land reform and land management can be summarised as a commitment to existing forms of traditional (tribal) tenure, and to a continuation of the traditional authority role in allocating land within existing traditional (tribal) areas."* (McIntosh *et al* 1995)

Although there is still considerable ambivalence among – and about – traditional authorities in the provinces, many would prefer land reform to extend the forms of tenure over which they have authority in order to expand their areas of influence.

Notwithstanding the political power play in KwaZulu-Natal, the Eastern Cape and Northern Province, the commitment on the part of many chiefs to traditional tenure arises from a genuine concern for welfare and equity. Their view is that they hold land in trust for their people. They allocate land to people on the basis of 'citizenship' – which may be kin derived and/or bought – and thereafter give consideration to equity.

Their actual practices, however, are often clouded by corruption, patronage and, increasingly, the influence of market forces as they slip between the traditional and modern systems to sell the land they hold in trust for personal profit and to consolidate their power base.

Everywhere there is increased pressure on existing holdings arising from the combined effects of natural population growth, generalised land hunger, the poor financial state of traditional authority areas and the struggle by chiefs to retain or extend their authority. The general tendencies regarding land are a reduction in plot size, the conversion of arable holdings and grazing land into residential sites, and the allocation of residential land without an accompanying arable holding.

These processes are typical across the country, although many variations arise from specific conditions in each locality. In KwaZulu-Natal, for instance, an exception to the tendency towards smaller plot sizes occurs in areas where sugar and timber outgrower schemes have been introduced by large corporations.

> *"Although land holders planted sugar and timber on their existing land holdings, there has been some agglomeration...from the increased value of land because it is under a commercial crop."* (McIntosh *et al* 1995)

Land has been freed up and reorganised through a range of actions, including pressure on land holders who have not been making full use of their holdings, confiscation of land from people opposed to the introduction of cane, and patronage.

> Absolute landlessness is less common in the congested former reserves than it is in white owned commercial areas

Land allocation outcomes are far from egalitarian. However, popular pressure to allocate land to everyone means that traditional authorities do have to pay some attention to the land needs of the least socially or politically powerful. The consequence is that although there is mounting landlessness, absolute landlessness is less common in the congested former reserves than it is in historically white owned commercial areas.

Most areas under traditional authorities do have sets of rules and established practices regarding the use of land, but they are increasingly difficult to enforce as a result of overcrowding, overstocking and weak administrative capacity. Traditional authorities spend considerable time resolving disputes which arise from these pressures rather than engaging in land management or protecting the environment. And even where individual chiefs have played vigorously interventionist roles to ensure proper land management, countervailing pressures have made it impossible for them to enforce particular patterns of land use. In fact, preference for weak traditional authority land administration has been generated through rejection of such controls.

For many traditional leaders, problems of land management derive from land shortages linked to historical dispossession

Seeking more land

For many traditional leaders, the problems of land management derive from land shortages which are inextricably linked to historical dispossession. It is their view that the only way to resolve disputes and poor land use practices is by restoring land as well as making new land available.

At the time of the research, there was some uncertainty among traditional leaders as to how land could be returned. However, many felt it would be best to bring land under traditional tenure, in order to confirm traditional authority control over access to land. As the procedures of land reform have become more clear, it has become evident that traditional authorities are making use of all the avenues it opens up.

Numerous traditional authorities in the various provinces are actively looking for more land. Many have already identified or could identify land which was formerly theirs but passed into the possession of white farmers or different arms of the state – including nature conservation authorities and the military – or became urban residential centres.

The Baralong Ba Ratshidi traditional authority in North West province is a case in point. The authority has submitted a restitution claim which covers the entire town of Mmabatho, and the local university and military base.

The Manenzhe community of former Venda is currently filing a claim for lost land which is divided into three categories: private farms, government owned buffer zones used by the military and police, and areas of state land bought by the former Venda government from white farmers and then leased to black farmers, none of them from Manenzhe.

Amakhosi are also effectively accessing land through the redistribution programme, especially in areas where it is difficult to separate socially identified strata such as former labour tenants and former farm workers from the political complex of which they are part. In KwaZulu-Natal, for example, they are using their capacity to institutionally underwrite applications for land in return for political allegiance and potential authority over land that is acquired.

Traditional versus modern

Traditional authorities, as a system, are caught in the contradictions of modernity. Hypothetically it is conceivable that land could be transferred to traditional authorities – as long as land is made available for traditional uses such as grazing, cropping and residential purposes on a micro scale, and as long as it is transferred in significant quantities.

> *"Until such time as the population pressures which are presently felt in many existing tribal holdings build up on reallocated lands, such allocation procedures might be sustainable. The mechanisms for managing such holdings are well known, simple and affordable."* (McIntosh *et al* 1995)

The institution of traditional authorities would be reinforced and maintained even if disputes arose, because disputes tend to focus on the conduct of particular individuals rather than on the institution of chieftaincy.

However, allocation practices are likely to be difficult to sustain on land made available for urban development or commercial agriculture. In urban fringe settlements, where social forces are diverse and kinship relations fragile, the weak authority of traditional institutions succumbs to the sway of powerful individuals who take and maintain control over the allocation of residential sites with the assistance of informal armed forces and party political patronage (Xaba 1994).

Many amakhosi are actively looking for more land through restitution and redistribution

Similarly, the commercialisation of agriculture impinges negatively on the powers and legitimacy of the traditional authority system. This is because commercial agriculture entrenches particular kinds of land rights which conflict with traditional rights, and which thereby change the nature of – as well as escalate the need for – dispute resolution.

These tensions are very evident in the district study area of Mhlatuze catchment in KwaZulu-Natal, where there are cane and timber outgrower schemes. There the meagre administrative resources of traditional authorities are stretched to the limit, and the authorities are barely able to cope with the high incidence of land disputes.

Traditional authority is being undermined by urban development and commercial agriculture

Commercialisation also increases social stratification. It creates a new class whose authority is sourced in freehold rights which encourage the accumulation of land and wealth, and simultaneously escalate landlessness. This class – through its wealth, demand for freehold tenure and capacity to mobilise political resources – poses a serious threat to the position and status of traditional authorities as individuals and as a system.

Traditional authorities are likely to respond to these challenges in various ways, but inevitably in ways which are likely to undermine the integrity of the system itself.

Most predictably, they are likely to alienate concessions to themselves and/or other wealthy individuals – at the expense of the ethic of the system of communal tenure. They may also resist an approach to land reform which centres on the development of rural service centres, if this process of urbanisation undermines their power base.

The position of women

Patriarchal practices are also being undermined, both by the inability of the traditional system to provide adequately for people's needs and by the possibilities opened up by the existence of alternatives.

Traditionally, land is allocated to men who in turn allocate it to their wives to use. Widows cannot formally acquire land in their own right, but they can inherit land. Thus, even though land rights are mediated – usually through sons – some women can and do become independent producers in the system.

Significantly, numerous successful small cane growers are widows, which suggests that the difficulties of surviving in the present day traditional system as a widow have forced many actively to seek alternatives which challenge their status as women and widows.

There is a powerful lobby for women to have access to land in their own right, and for those rights not to depend on marital status. There are clear advantages of such a change for some women, although there are men and women who clearly support men's control over land rights because it underpins the institution of marriage in many rural areas.

Moving from mediated to direct land rights within the traditional authorities system as it is now might leave some women with access to less land than they currently have.

Acquiring secure rights to land will be a gain for many women, potentially opening up new routes of access to land and income. But it is unlikely to be sufficient to counter the cluster of pressures which give rise to gendered rural poverty, particularly the already evident erosion of support obligations to non-working women with children in male headed households.

In many respects trends in the gender dynamic within traditional rural households mirror institutional trends within the traditional authorities system.

Possibly more serious for women's land access, and rural land access in general, is for women's land rights to be affixed to inalienable individual rights – as they are in white owned commercial areas. Most will lose the little they have, and many will have slender prospects of regaining land through the market.

Civics and tribal authorities in the Eastern Cape

In many areas of former Ciskei, where civics emerged to take on some of the responsibilities of local government – especially matters relating to land administration – tense dual power exists between them and tribal authorities. There, rural people may be prepared to accommodate chiefs in a new form of local government.

In former Transkei, popular dissatisfaction is not as widespread and traditional authorities have fairly strong support in some areas, even though their legitimacy was challenged and alternative structures such as civics emerged.

Meanwhile, in 'black spots' in the former Border Corridor, traditional authorities have collapsed. Many have been replaced by locally initiated structures which float in limbo in a sea of institutional confusion, duplication and inefficiency.

Women in traditional authority areas could lose land by gaining land rights

A future role

> The demand for land by traditional authorities is likely to mobilise support from large numbers of poor rural dwellers

Traditional authorities and the traditional tenure system have provided affordable access to land for a large number of people and a simple and enduring system for administering it.

Nevertheless, heed needs to be taken of popular experience of and feelings towards the traditional authorities system. The message is mixed and attitudes are not homogenous, geographically or socially.

In many parts of the country chiefs and headmen have lost legitimacy through a combination of abuse of power, complicity with apartheid and a failure to deliver even elementary support and services.

At the same time, tolerance of traditional authorities endures even in conditions of adverse experience. This is clearly evident in Northern Province, the North West, Mpumalanga, Free State and KwaZulu-Natal, as well as in the Eastern Cape, which exemplifies some of the range of conditions prevailing.

There is a vacuum around local authority and governance in rural areas throughout the country. In many areas there are multiple organisations and even systems, all of which have been competing for legitimacy and space in new local governments.

Elsewhere, community trusts and other stopgap measures have been introduced to fill the vacuum. While they have been developed to meet particular needs, they are not alternative forms of land administration and cannot substitute for government.

If alternative mechanisms for administering communal land are to be developed, their success will depend on the emergence of effective systems of local government to provide support and services. This, in turn, will require a considerable injection of financial and human resources, which seems unlikely at present.

The central role traditional authorities play in allocating land is generally negatively perceived. In most communities in most provinces, traditional authorities are not regarded as the best agents to distribute land or stimulate development, although there are differences in view between communities and by age and sex.

The Land Reform Research Programme's National Report found that among people needing land, 21,2% felt that traditional authorities were best placed to allocate land, 41% felt they should not allocate land, and the rest thought they could be involved in allocating land but should not be the sole agency.

The allocation nettle is one which the Government will have to grasp. There are constitutional and legislative provisions which further inform the debate. In reality, communities are likely to resort to what is known, what is in their capacity and what has credibility. Traditional authorities, local government and other land allocation institutions are among the options open to them.

CHAPTER EIGHT

WOMEN

The Land Reform Research Programme largely concentrated on the differential needs for land between men and women, with only a limited focus on the crucial question of the relations of power that determine women's participation in, access to and control over land and other resources. Nevertheless, it yielded some interesting results.

Women see access to land as central to their role in social reproduction and the domestic economy

As a social category, women are evidently interested in land. Their interest cuts across social strata, and is concentrated among the landless and micro producers. Women are also present in surplus, commercialising and established commercial production, and are only notably absent from the corporate sector.

Land is important to women as a resource. Especially, it:

> *"...represents an opportunity for women to meet a variety of needs, including those which are socially identified as primarily their responsibility."* (Walker 1994)

Most women see access to land as central to their role in social reproduction – seeing to all their family's needs – and the domestic economy.

Their demand for land commonly centres on securing a place to live, providing fuel and thatch, and supplementing food for household consumption. Social reproduction is the common denominator underlying women's land demand.

At the same time, women's use of and interest in productive land is differentiated by a cluster of factors which combine in a range of ways. Especially important are prevailing practices and forms of agricultural production, the way women are integrated into formal and informal employment, their household structure and the effects of restrictive legal and customary regimes.

For example, in the Karoo in the Eastern Cape, where extensive commercial livestock farming predominates, land needs related to production do not feature prominently among women. Many expressed the need for residential land. They also articulated a need for land for fuel and some women were interested in poultry farming and vegetable production on communal gardens.

In conditions where there is a keen interest in stock farming among men, relatively few women aspire to become stock farmers – even though some of them own animals. Significantly, women who own stock are not part of stock owners organisations where these exist.

And generally, community based organisations that have been established around land needs tend to focus on stock farming or what have been termed 'men's land needs' (Eastern Cape, Karoo Sub-division 1995).

The experience of the Eastern Cape – that few women perceive themselves as or are interested in becoming 'farmers', stock or arable – can be generalised to most rural based women throughout the country and needs some explanation, especially since women make up a large proportion of micro producers and appear to be more interested in preserving an agricultural subsistence base than men.

Part of the answer to why they want land and continue to work it lies in a realistic assessment of their extremely disadvantaged position in and experience of a hostile job market (Walker 1994).

Women are more likely to be unemployed than men, with the severity of their job position masked by the way official unemployment rates are figured: Horn (1994) points out that the Central Statistical Service calculates the rate of male unemployment on the basis of 95% of the adult male population, while the female rate is calculated from 55 % of the adult female population.

Few women are interested in becoming 'farmers', stock or arable, but they need land for residence, fuel and micro farming

When they are employed, women tend to be drawn into the very bottom and often the worst end of the formal economy – domestic service and commercial agriculture. In commercial agriculture, with the exception of the Western Cape, women are invariably employed as casual or part-time workers, earning small sums of money – R7 to R10 a day – for limited periods at irregular and indeterminate intervals. Where they are employed as part of the full-time workforce they earn, on average, 75% of male full-time equivalent wages.

A range of factors, particularly sectoral restructuring, declining levels of employment and drought, suggest that the employment position of women in agriculture and in the job market at large, has deteriorated in many parts of the country.

Extreme disadvantage in employment, law and custom make agriculture less attractive for women

Thus, land for agricultural purposes is one element of a package of survival strategies in conditions of extremely constrained choices which, possibly for many women, is not regarded as the most rewarding in terms of income generation (Walker 1994).

In part, the reason why few women aspire to become farmers is to be found in the negative weight of legal and customary discrimination against them. Especially in rural areas, their rights, status, authority and representation is overwhelmingly mediated by their relationship to men – whether they fall within the traditional authorities system, live in black owned freehold areas or live and work in commercial agriculture.

While the research shows that many women actively participate in and reinforce male mediation, there are countervailing pressures from segments of women who want unmediated property rights and equal status and authority as men.

In the traditional authorities system, land continues to be allocated to men who in turn allocate it to their wives to use. Since 1987 in KwaZulu-Natal, for example, the law has allowed women household heads to acquire land in their own right, although there is little evidence that this provision has become practice. Rather, customary mediation prevails. Most women who have access to land 'in their own right' are widows who inherited the land on the death of their husbands.

This pattern of land allocation extends into modern land transfers taking place in the current land reform programme. Thus, the labour tenant community that has acquired the farm Gannahoek in KwaZulu-Natal:

> *"...has very conservative feelings about holding and transferring land, and it has been difficult to persuade them to grant rights to women. The preference is for male heads of households to hold land on behalf of their families."* (Cross *et al* 1995)

A similar pattern of mediated access is played out in what used to be Coloured Reserve Areas such as Slangspruit in the southern

Cape and even in freehold tenure areas like Cornfields in KwaZulu-Natal, where women can and do own land in their own right.

In Slangspruit, while there is a long tradition of women owning land, less than 18% of residential plots are registered in the names of women residents, most of whom are widows. In Cornfields, although land tenure is not regulated formally by traditional leaders and customary law, in practice women are subject to a complex of both systems. Once again, the women who hold land are widows, and the flexibility around women's access to land is motivated by efforts to keep land within original land owning families.

Reluctance to allow women access to land in their own right is intimately tied up with maintaining patriarchal inheritance rules and rights:

> *"Male children maintain the family name...female members of households are always bound to be married. Therefore, if they inherit property and thereafter get married, the property of the deceased is left in the hands of a stranger."* (Cross *et al* 1995)

The core assumption underpinning widows' rights to land is that it is transitional: a temporary arrangement in the transfer of authority from husbands to sons. The custom of a brother or male relative inheriting the property of a deceased, including the wife of the deceased – termed *ukungena* in Zulu – is less frequent nowadays.

But it is fairly common practice across a range of communities for a widow to hold land until she dies, at which time it passes on to the male heir, or to hold land until the heir comes of age. As an intercessor, she rarely if ever has full authority over the land. Decisions are taken in consideration of, if not with deference to, the 'real' heir.

The lack of access to and rights over land among African women reflects a still strongly patriarchal society

While many women strongly assert their right to inherit land, research in KwaZulu-Natal (Walker 1994; Cross *et al* 1995) and the southern Cape (Southern Cape District Case Studies 1995) suggests that they hold a contrary view about their daughters' rights to inherit or gain unmediated access to land.

Most uphold a son's prior claim to property over that of a daughter's as natural and right. They support the general opinion that daughters inherit as a last resort, when there are no sons and no other close male relative. These attitudes sharply reflect the contradictions in women's standpoints to male power as well as their uncertainties about how far equality between men and women should go.

Women have virtually no access to farm based resources, especially to housing, health and child care

These commonly held views, however, are also likely to be modified by practical circumstances. Thus, in the former Transkei, older unmarried women seem to have been able to gain access to land in their own right through mediation by a male family member (Van Averbeke 1995).

It appears that slim prospects for marriage and the burden of mature, unmarried children on poorly resourced households with limited land access has forced some change in land access rights in practice and is a pressure behind the demand for land (Marcus 1995).

Although widowhood is one of the main routes by which women access land, it is itself contradictory. Widowhood often means loss of (regular) income, it may entail loss of land and it often affects women's social standing. But in conditions where parallel authority and rights systems are operating, it can create openings for women to act on their own behalf.

On freehold title land, such as Cornfields, female headed households – mostly widowed women – are investing more heavily than men in membership of a trust created to manage newly acquired land (Walker 1994).

Corporate outgrower schemes provide a similar opening. In KwaZulu-Natal, an estimated 65% of small cane growers are women, of whom a significant proportion are widows. Widows grow cane in their own right as they are allowed to register independently, without male authorisation.

Their position compares starkly with women who, as wives, are legal minors whose economic independence is inhibited by the refusal of their husbands to allow them to sign contracts to join small grower schemes – or when they are allowed, are robbed of the benefits of their labours because the men sign contracts expecting to take the money while the women do all the work (Vaughan in Schrire R *Wealth or Poverty* 1992).

Male mediation of female rights is also typical in the commercial farming sector. Women have virtually no access to farm based resources, especially to housing, health and child care, or to land use rights other than through their husbands, fathers or brothers.

Lack of access to resources is further conditioned by women's willingness to do seasonal, casual or domestic work for the farmer employer. They are subjected to dual patriarchies which operate domestically and in the workplace, and which intertwine by virtue of the fact that work and home are physically located at the same site.

From the bottom of a long history of mediated rights to land, it is not surprising to find that many women do not perceive themselves as or aspire to be farmers in their own right. This does not mean that they are not land users and have no need for land.

Rather, it suggests that the emphasis placed on commercialising farmers needs to be reviewed in the light of women's needs and experiences. Moreover, establishing some degree of economic independence for some women is only part of a process of very incomplete change in gender relations. Rarely does it translate into a direct or explicit challenge of patriarchal authority and control.

In most rural communities, community politics and local governance are still largely structured by an overarching ideology and practice of male authority. Rarely do women participate in the committee or traditional governance structures of community life, even though they are often deeply involved in community affairs and actively participate in social networks beyond the household.

Where opportunities arise for them to make stronger claims, they are generally hesitant and doubtful of the legitimacy of their presence as women. They are held back by customary practices, prejudice and their own ambivalences about assuming different roles (Walker 1994) as much as by domestic responsibilities and integration into a distinctly female gendered network of social interaction (Eastern Cape: Karoo Sub-Division 1995).

> The emphasis placed on commercialising farmers needs to be reviewed in the light of women's needs and experiences

Nevertheless, there is a challenge implicit in the tension between acceptance of the ideology of 'official rural patriarchy' and the practices of daily living, which often generate a strong sense among women that they are oppressed by men and the institutions around them.

Whether this challenge will become explicit depends on whether there are structural and institutional supports to back it up. The only way it is likely to be translated from an individual to a collective and sustained review of patriarchal power is through directed incremental support, which is focused to address perceived needs but which simultaneously opens up spaces for women to redefine their rights, roles and responsibilities.

PART TWO
STRUCTURAL CONSIDERATIONS

CHAPTER NINE

THE COMMERCIAL AGRICULTURE SECTOR

> 55 000 white farmers own 102 million hectares while 1,2 million micro farmers share just 17 million hectares

Opening up the commercial agriculture sector to new black entrants will be neither swift nor simple, since for most of the 20th Century the Government's agricultural policies have served to suppress and undermine black commercial farmers.

Within a generation of the 1913 Natives (Land) Act, the viability of the small but vibrant black commercial farming sector had been eroded.

Excluded from markets, credit facilities and cooperatives, denied subsidies and soft loans, ignored by extension schemes, bypassed by infrastructural development, and penalised by racialised rights in property, black farmers did not stand a chance against the rising political power of white farmers.

The deracialisation of land holding in South Africa is an urgent imperative, given that 55 000 white farmers currently own 102 million hectares of land, in bitter contrast to the 1,2 million micro farmers who share just 17 million hectares in the former homelands.

There are two potential routes for opening up participation in commercial agriculture by black South Africans. The first is for small and large scale farmers to join the ranks of the commercial sector, and the second is for farm workers to become part owners of the farms on which they work through share equity schemes.

However, agrarian reform in South Africa on the eve of the 21st Century raises issues beyond the racial profile of land holding. The extent of sectoral linkages is illustrative: who deals with whom and on what terms.

Since 1993, the powers of the marketing control boards have been scaled down dramatically. Yet even if this process continues along

The red meat industry

Until very recently, the red meat industry was regulated by a tight framework governing production, distribution and meat processing. Regulations have eased, but the Meat Board continues to control the supply and price of red meat.

By regulating imports and using imported red meat to meet shortfalls in supply from local commercial farmers, the Meat Board effectively blocks the entry of small scale and intermittent producers into the big urban markets. Moreover, by being able to point to the ready availability of imported meat, bodies like the Meat Board have been able to veto the establishment of new abattoirs in localities suited to small scale African stock farmers. As a result the meat market continues to favour established interests.

The red meat marketing system and its associated agents, registration requirements, health regulations, permits and quotas have tended to favour large producers, feedlotters and vertically integrated businesses within the industry.

The industry is dominated by three large companies – Vleissentraal, Foodcorp (formerly Kanhym) and Imperial Cold Storage. All have significant interests in feedlots, whose prominence as major suppliers of meat nationally has risen in recent years.

Less susceptible to climatic variations, feedlotters have gained tremendous market share through the quota system, and potentially represent a significant competitive obstacle to small scale producers wanting to break into the lucrative urban market. Smaller intermittent sellers of stock have lost considerable market share to the feedlotters (Fleming 1994b).

Stringent health regulations constitute a further barrier to market entry for small scale producers. The main retail food stores prefer to buy from Abacor abattoirs, presumably not wanting to risk receiving lower quality meat from unclassified abattoirs – and strict quotas determine throughput at abattoirs, again discriminating against intermittent and small scale producers (Marcus 1995b).

Even if the red meat industry is deregulated significantly, it is likely that the existing channels of processing and distribution will continue to dominate for some considerable time. Ironically, the power of the major players was amassed in a highly protective environment which was developed to serve the interests of farmers: that regulatory environment is being dismantled at precisely the time when new black farmers are entering the sector, and are in need of support and protection.

Regulations that protected white farmers are being dismantled at precisely the time when new black farmers need them its present course and the regulatory powers of state structures which protected established producers are cut back further, there is no assurance that opportunities for market entry by new producers will improve significantly.

Agrarian reform encompasses more than improved access by black farmers to land holding, and raises questions such as who has access to applied research, extension services, potential markets and accessible transport services.

If black farmers are to progress beyond the margins of the commercial farming sector, questions need to be asked about who the food retailers and manufacturers trade with and on what terms, the volume and grade of commodities they demand and the kind of inputs and financial servicing this requires (Williams 1993).

The powers of marketing control boards have been scaled down, but this does not ensure improved opportunities for new producers

Commercial farming definitions

The use of the term 'commercial farmer' in the South African context conjures up the image of a large scale, white producer. This type of producer usually sells crops through cooperatives or official marketing channels, and may often be particularly geared to production for the export market. However, this is an unhelpfully narrow interpretation and, as we argue here, it excludes a range of other farmers.

It is worth returning to the definition of what is meant by commercial farming. Clearly, it is envisaged as a situation in which a farmer produces more than is required for subsistence and is thus able to sell surplus production. Thus the definition of a commercial farmer must be directly linked to the contribution that the farmer makes to the supply of marketed agricultural production.

Using this wider definition, we can incorporate the activities of small scale, black farmers, especially women. These farmers are often important suppliers of livestock and crops in the rural and peri-urban markets of South Africa.

Vegetables, in particular, is an area where small scale farmers produce and market a surplus. For policy purposes, it is useful to recognise the commercial nature of this production and its importance for meeting the food needs of households.

This book has tended to use the narrower definition, without losing sight of the wider scope of production.

Maize producers maintain dominance

Just under 3,5 million hectares of highveld cropland is planted with maize each year. Two distinct types of maize are produced: white maize is milled to produce maize meal, the staple food of most South Africans, while yellow maize is used to make animal feeds. How maize is produced and traded has a direct impact on what South Africans eat, and what their food costs them.

Until April 30, 1995, maize was marketed through a statutory single channel marketing scheme operated by the Maize Board. Farmers were only allowed to sell their maize through the Maize Board, which set the price. The price was uniform across the country, and made no allowance for quality or distance from the market. Maize imports and exports were carefully regulated to protect local producers from any advantages enjoyed by overseas producers, as a result of better growing conditions or government support.

Maize farmers dominate the Maize Board, through their powerful producer organisation Nampo, which represents the interests primarily of large scale producers. Nampo members also feature prominently among the directors of the country's big summer grain cooperatives.

Actual handling of maize regulated by the Maize Board was through cooperatives such as the Eastern Transvaal Cooperative (OTK) and Sentraal-Wes. These cooperatives own most of the grain silos, channel credit to maize farmers and supply them with inputs such as seed, fertiliser, machinery and fuel. They are involved in milling and animal feed production.

Since the early 1980s, the cooperatives have become a distinct form of agribusiness, run by professional managers and engaged in a range of business activities. They have taken over smaller cooperatives, diversified into a range of downstream activities which use maize and maize products (milling, animal feeds, poultry production and feedlots), and are now diversifying into processing and distributing other agricultural products. Cooperatives own most bulk handling and storage facilities, which gives them a powerful base from which to dictate the terms on which maize is traded.

Within a few years, OTK and other large cooperatives will probably transform themselves into public companies listed on the Johannesburg Stock Exchange.

The cooperatives wield enormous power over their members: they provide production credit, generally on condition that farmers buy their inputs from them and sell their crops to them. Although most (excluding OTK) now accept black farmers as members, the cooperatives' policies favour large scale farmers. Increasingly they are turning their backs on those they perceive as a bad debt risk.

Far reaching rural restructuring is needed, but it is unlikely that land reform alone will provide the necessary impetus

The deregulation of maize marketing is only partial. It means an end to monopoly marketing and the price fixing powers of the Maize Board, as the Board now operates a floor (or minimum) price system. It retains control over exports and imports. Surplus removal and export pool schemes are still being operated by the Maize Board, and continue to be dominated by Nampo and the cooperatives.

Diminished state regulation of the maize industry could reduce competition, rather than strengthen it, between the main producers. What deregulation has given rise to is a marketing system where agents of the major producers can operate a virtual cartel, with dire implications for affordability for most maize consumers. Although it is not yet clear who will emerge as the leading maize traders, it is very likely that the cooperatives will dominate.

The first buying price announced by the Maize Board under the new trading regime led to a significant bonus for maize producers and cooperatives, and an alarming increase in the price of maize for consumers. Further increases are anticipated.

Apart from a handful of black commercial maize farmers, black people appear in the maize commodity chain primarily as consumers of maize meal, and as farm and factory workers. Maize production in the former bantustans totalled just 3% of the total national maize output, almost all of it for home consumption.

The large maize producers entrenched their dominance with the support of the grain cooperatives. With the large cooperatives restructuring themselves aggressively as agribusinesses, it is unlikely that aspirant black commercial farmers will receive similar support.

(Summarised from Nic Amin and Henry Bernstein (1995) 'The Political Economy of Deregulation in South Africa: The Maize and Red Meat Industries'. Paper delivered at the 'Agrarian Questions: The Politics of Farming', conference at Wageningen Agricultural University, Amo, May 22-24, 1995.)

Black people appear in the maize commodity chain primarily as consumers of maize meal, and as farm and factory workers

Overview

The commercial farming sector has enjoyed more than half a century of special treatment, and has probably received more from government than any other sector. Cost-plus prices, exemption from labour legislation, assured markets, cheap low risk credit and generous subsidies kept farmers happy and secured the farming sector's political support in rural constituencies loaded in favour of the National Party. The cost to South Africa's economy has been high.

Simon Fiske sums up the result succinctly:

> *"Most farmers have little experience of taking their own decisions, farm workers have limited training and few social rights, farming systems have become monolithic and most of the infrastructure, such as abattoirs, is too large, badly run and in the wrong place."* (*Effective Farming*, October 1995)

Far reaching rural restructuring is called for – but it is unlikely that the land reform programme will provide the necessary impetus.

Less than 15% of South Africa's land area is arable, and just 3% is regarded as high potential land: its soils are fragile and highly susceptible to erosion. These facts heighten the importance of making the best use of good land to maximise internal food security and export potential.

All too often, government policies have subsidised bad farming practices – excessive reliance on monoculture, intensive application of agro-chemicals and production of crops ill suited to prevailing rainfall and soil conditions.

As the country's population grows, it becomes even more important to work the land in a way that is ecologically responsible, cost effective and ensures food security.

The agricultural sector plays a significant role in South Africa's economy as a major income generator and employer, despite the fact that its contribution to Gross Domestic Product is just 5%. Because of extensive forward and backward linkages, reduced or improved agricultural performance has a direct and significant influence on the national economy. As commercial agriculture is presently structured it employs a large workforce which, after declining in the 1980s, has now stabilised.

> Agricultural servicing has focused on the commercial sector at the cost of broadening the producer base and supporting small scale farmers

The commercial agricultural sector is in the hands of roughly 55 000 commercial farmers and agri-businesses. Fewer than 1 500 of them are black farmers. Within the commercial sector, productive output is concentrated: according to a recent study, 25% of commercial farmers produce more than 80% of output (Van Rooyen 1995).

Agricultural servicing – including physical infrastructure, extension, financing, cooperatives and marketing support – has focused exclusively on the commercial sector. Previous government policies prioritised national food security through commercialisation at the cost of broadening the producer base and supporting small scale farmers.

A blanket approach to produce marketing has inhibited the development of small scale agri-business

National food security has been achieved. Self sufficiency indices show that grain production has an index of 150, where 100 represents national food self sufficiency, horticultural production has an index of 132 and livestock production 98 (quoted in Van Rooyen 1995). Yet household food security levels are shockingly low. An estimated 60% of the population lives below the minimum living level, and less than a quarter of micro producers generate their own food requirements.

The existing structure of commercial agriculture has boosted productivity at the cost of rising unemployment, landlessness and poverty, and has contributed to the decay of small platteland towns.

Marketing of produce has been regulated tightly within a statutory framework, with farmers facing fines and penalties for circumventing the controls. The single channel maize marketing system, for example, set up a single national pricing system which rewarded all producers equally, regardless of crop quality, distance from the market or volume.

This blanket approach inhibited the development of small scale agri-businesses, like grain mills and processing plants, in outlying areas. As a result, rural areas have missed out on the small scale adjunct enterprises which add value to local produce and provide jobs. Centralised processing has played its part in the decline of platteland towns which, in the past, functioned as rural service centres.

If agriculturally related enterprises are to be established to ensure that their benefits are enjoyed locally, considerable investment will be needed to establish or improve supportive infrastructure. Yet under free market conditions, local value added enterprises in rural areas are likely to take decades to establish and become secure. Recreating a mix of rural enterprises will entail considerable investment and even a preparedness to incur losses until profitability is achieved.

Despite records dating back for over a century which detail erratic rainfall patterns within broad cycles of wet and dry years, government support policies have treated drought as an aberration rather than a normal characteristic of a semi-arid country.

Following from this, drought aid schemes focused on the consequences of drought, rather than on helping farmers manage the risk of drought more constructively by switching to less vulnerable production systems.

Cheap – subsidised – credit has proved very costly to South Africa. It has distorted land and input prices, spurred mechanisation and contributed to high levels of debt which many farmers are struggling to service. One reason for the latter is that low interest rates have, ironically, encouraged farmers to default on subsidised loans, since they can get a higher return on their money by spending it elsewhere. Subsidies and tax breaks have also encouraged farmers to increase farm size and substitute labour with machinery.

Since the late 1980s there has been a profound shift away from regulation, in response to government's determination to wean farmers from expensive subsidies and force them to become more responsive to the market and more competitive in the face of 'liberalised' international trade. Unfortunately for farmers, this shift has coincided with rising input costs, high inflation and several seasons of severe drought. The result has been an extremely painful period of transition.

Farm workers have borne the brunt of these problems. According to Development Bank of Southern Africa records, employment on farms fell 25% between 1985 and 1992 and has dropped steadily since. Nearly half of Northern Province's 60 000 farm workers were laid off early in the summer of 1995/1996 because of cost price squeezes and late rain (*Business Day* November 17, 1995). The results of these cutbacks include profound destabilisation in many rural areas, and rising crime.

> Deregulation has coincided with rising input costs, inflation and drought. Farm workers have suffered, with massive cuts to permanent jobs

The Government is adamant that commercial agriculture will have to face up to the challenges of economic pricing and competitiveness like any other sector, and that the days of special treatment are over. Moreover, government genuinely has little to offer commercial farmers in the face of competing claims from housing, education, health and other sectors.

Nonetheless, some price supports remain. Farmers are still being supported to grow crops ill suited to drought prone areas, and medium and long term interest rates are still subsidised. A number of mainly political factors explain this. National Party control of the Agriculture Ministry in the Government of National Unity has discouraged a significant rethink on agricultural policy at this stage.

Also, the Government faces a profound dilemma. It is under acute political pressure to change the racial map of land holding in South Africa. It faces a vocal lobby of conservative white farmers clamouring to defend the perks and subsidies they have enjoyed for half a century. Equally, it faces an impoverished – and numerically powerful – black rural populace in dire need of support and relief.

Supporting white agriculture sustains a form of safety net for rural people

The Government is all too aware that it currently lacks the means to launch a rural welfare support programme. For all its faults and problems, continued support of white commercial agriculture does sustain a form of safety net for rural people, however compromised. The Government has been obliged to back down on minimum wage policies in the face of farmer organisations' threats that enforcing higher wages for farm labourers will simply lead to mass dismissals.

Commercial agriculture is in an awkward position. In order to survive in the 1990s, farmers are cutting overheads to a minimum, focusing especially on wage saving activities by reducing the number of permanent workers, increasing the use of seasonal labour, and keeping wages low, which drought and labour legislation have provided justification for. But there is a limit to how much commercial farmers can trim their workforce: the closer they are to that limit, the less their leverage with the Government.

Promoting land access

Improving land holding for a sector of the black population which currently has limited or no access to land will only transform that populace into a class of small scale farmers if the necessary support infrastructure is made available and effective – and if the recipients wish to farm.

There is a growing perception, especially among commercial farmers, that the allocation of land for poverty alleviation and the splitting up of large units of land for allocation to small scalc farmers is a 'bantustan solution', and runs the risk of replicating in commercial farming areas precisely the conditions which prevail in former bantustans (Vawda 1995; McIntosh 1995).

Promoting access to land for aspirant black farmers is particularly complex. There seems to be a pervasive assumption that the land reform programme will broaden access to the agricultural sector, and thereby lay the basis for the transformation of that sector in South Africa (White Paper on Agriculture 1995).

The basic land settlement grant

The R15 000 basic land settlement grant amounts to little more than a handout when made available to individual households or small groups of rural people with limited ambitions. It is unlikely to provide them with the means to start farming on a scale that will generate marketable surpluses.

But when made available to a large number of households, its impact can be dramatic. In a pioneering farm worker equity scheme in the Mpumalanga Lowveld in early 1996, 600 farm workers pooled their R15 000 grants to purchase a 50% stake in a high potential export fruit farm. Their stake in a highly profitable venture producing a range of sub-tropical fruits and vegetables is likely to reward them with substantial dividends which, in the short term, can be used to improve their housing, education levels and prospects.

Emergent farmers fall between the Department of Land Affairs's land reform programme, aimed at the poorest of the poor, and the Department of Agriculture's small farmer support schemes, which presuppose that farmers already have access to land.

But the R15 000 grant, for which they qualify, can be used innovatively as an entry point into a range of farming options – leasing, share cropping and so on – from which they can leverage their way into more permanent land holdings. Used creatively, the basic grant amounts to considerably more than a short term welfare payment for those willing to exploit the opportunities which exist in the commercial farming sector.

Effective support infrastructure will be needed if improving land holding to black people is to lead to successful small scale farming

Alongside this, many believe that there is enormous potential for developing efficient, labour absorptive small holder agriculture (Vawda). Both the African National Congress's (ANC's) agricultural policy document and the Government's White Paper on Agriculture stress the importance of promoting efficient small scale farming which ensures household food security and boosts employment in a range of infrastructural and off-farm enterprises.

However, the Department of Land Affairs has been careful to stress that the focus of its land reform activities is to address the injustices of forced removals, provide land for the landless, provide greater security of tenure and address basic needs.

Agricultural development, although critical, is outside the Department's brief, and it has neither the resources nor the funding to support a full scale farmer development programme. That responsibility falls to the Department of Agriculture, which has committed itself to reorienting its focus and policies in support of smaller scale farming. Improving access to farmland is not part of its mandate.

According to the RDP, restructuring the agricultural sector consists of spreading the ownership base, encouraging small scale farming, and increasing production and employment. Responsibility for facilitating the spread of ownership and improving access to commercial farm land is not specified.

Access to farm land beyond the allocation of small parcels for poverty relief is likely to remain beyond the reach of most people

Black commercial farmers seem to have fallen between two stools: they are not being targeted by land reform policies beyond a minimum settlement grant, and agricultural support mechanisms presuppose they have access to land.

Considerable attention is being paid to revising credit and finance mechanisms, to redirecting agricultural research towards crops suitable for risk prone farmers and to broadening the institutional infrastructure to provide support for a far wider farmer client base. Yet broadening access to farm land itself – beyond the allocation of small land parcels for basic poverty relief – is likely to remain beyond the reach of all but a small elite. This gap may reflect a trade-off between the ANC led Department of Land Affairs and the National Party led Department of Agriculture.

A matching grant scheme, below a ceiling which has yet to be specified, has been mooted to support the establishment of a new class of farmers. Even so, the limits of land purchase will be set by the ability of purchasers to service and repay their debts, and credit will be needed for a range of purposes including land, labour, infrastructure and production inputs.

The market in farm land is very active, with an estimated 4% of total land area – five million hectares – traded through the market annually (Van Rooyen 1995). But the high price of privately owned land is likely to limit the number of beneficiaries in a land reform *cum* agricultural development initiative.

Although considerable government funds have been budgeted for land purchase, it is unlikely that the Government will seek to purchase expensive high potential land when the benefits of finite resources can be spread far wider by trading off soil potential against surface area to some extent. For aspirant farmers and those wishing to extend their farming activities, land must first be made available to those who can pay for it.

Self evidently, the free market is not free, and one needs money to play (Levin 1994). Land prices vary enormously, depending on soil potential, rainfall, access to supplementary water sources, carrying capacity, proximity to markets, security and a host of other variables.

Sugar cane farming, for example, is being touted as an attractive option for farmers wanting to progress beyond micro production. However, the average price of land for sugar cane in northern KwaZulu-Natal is R14 000 per hectare, which puts the cost of a modest commercial cane farm at about R1 million. Depending on locality, viable land parcels suitable for mixed farming start from about R500 000, and the average is far in excess of that figure.

On a more positive note, the land lease market is very active: in 1988, the latest year for which data is available, nearly 20% of the total land area was leased (Van Rooyen 1995). Leasing may offer some scope for market entry.

Legal proscriptions on the sub-division of land have tended to inflate the purchase price of small farms. Abolishing the Sub-Division of Land Act will certainly bring more small land parcels onto the market and reduce the price of market entry. But sub-portions of existing farms which are sold may require substantial investment in infrastructure, which will add to the purchase price.

Aspirant purchasers who are able to mobilise the necessary finance to buy a farm then face the task of generating sufficient income to repay their loans. Agricultural operations have a low rate of cash generation – usually about 5% a year – and hence cash flows in the first five years are generally tightly constrained.

> The 20% of land expected to change hands over the next five years falls short of the Government's 30% target for restitution and redistribution

New farmers face a potentially crippling debt and interest burden unless they have cash reserves or other finance to get through this initial period, as well as additional finance to develop the farm to meet their production requirements. All too often, farms that come onto the market are offered for sale precisely because they are not commercially efficient, not fully developed, have fallen into disuse or are vulnerable to theft and other crime. Addressing these issues requires a heavy commitment of finance and labour (Vawda 1995).

It is a sad irony that the Agricultural Credit Board raised short term interest rates six percentage points in December 1995, at precisely the time when new black farmers were starting to look for production credit. Medium and long term rates are being maintained at 8%, against a prime lending rate of 18,5% and a Bankers' Acceptance rate of 14,15% in late 1995.

If 4% of total land area is traded annually, a total of 20% may be expected to change hands over the next five years on a willing-buyer-willing-seller basis. This falls short of the 30% target

The freeze on additional water for agriculture is likely to penalise new black farmers

Fruit and vegetable production

Horticulture offers great potential for small scale farmers. Provided water is available – lack of access to irrigable land is a powerful barrier to market entry – fresh produce can be cultivated intensively on small tracts of land. Despite intense population pressure, arable land has been found to be under utilised, especially in parts of Mpumalanga and KwaZulu-Natal, while grazing land is over utilised.

Horticultural crops are ideally suited to peri-urban and even urban production. Fruit, vegetables, high value herbs and spices and even tea can be grown profitably on a small scale, and can supplement household needs more satisfactorily than cash crops.

The most significant bottleneck for small scale horticulturists is market access. The market for fresh produce is highly competitive, and small scale growers can seldom exploit the economies of scale associated with forward linkages such as transportation, packaging and sale. Few emergent growers are able to compete successfully with the formal commercial sector, even when targeting the informal retail sector.

Quality and quantity of supply are the two most important factors determining commercial buyers' choice of supplier. While small scale farmers can compete on quality when harvesting, they often face difficulties meeting the required volumes on a continuous basis. Moreover, quality declines rapidly when farmers cannot market their produce rapidly, whether because of poor transport infrastructure or barriers to market access. Packaging is also important, and often small scale producers cannot meet the exacting requirements of urban consumers.

Fruit and vegetable wholesalers have elaborate networks of purchase and sales throughout the country, but unless small scale suppliers can meet their requirements for quality and continuous supply, most wholesalers prefer to buy from established producers.

A central commodity broking service linking intermittent producers with the major produce buyers might help small scale producers develop the expertise needed to trade in the increasingly competitive fruit and vegetable market.

which Land Affairs Minister Derek Hanekom has set for redistribution and restitution and, in any case, this amount does not address the needs of aspirant commercial farmers.

As Van Rooyen points out, this raises questions about how the remainder will be mobilised: government funds for land purchase are limited, and the Department of Land Affairs has emphasised that expropriation will only be used in extreme cases.

In view of the short term economic advantages of maintaining the *status quo* on white commercial farms, the resources made available to the Government's land reform programmes mean that most productive land will remain primarily in white hands for the forseeable future.

Water: the real constraint

Control over South Africa's water resources is even more concentrated in white hands than land. Increased ground water abstraction, proliferation of farm dams and major expansion of irrigation in the past three decades has meant that a relatively small number of land owners control the greater portion of the country's utilisable water (Forster 1995).

The Government is currently exploring a range of ways to revise existing water law and water allocations in the interests of greater equity. It has prioritised delivery of a basic water supply to all, and has frozen the allocation of further water to agriculture.

There is a clear and urgent need to improve the supply of potable water, especially to rural communities, but the freeze on additional water for agriculture is likely to penalise new black farmers, as commercial farmers with existing water rights will not readily forego those without compensation, and resolution of the compensation issue is a long way off.

> It is unlikely that land reform will have much impact on the structure of the agricultural sector

Rather than seeking ways to adjust the apportionment of water within the agricultural sector, the Department of Water Affairs has taken a firm policy decision against augmenting existing irrigation schemes or developing new irrigation infrastructure.

In view of this principled stance, it is likely that the productivity of aspirant commercial farmers will be determined, to a large extent, by their access to water. As the price of a farm is often determined by its water resources, farmers entering the land market will either have to raise sufficient capital to buy a well watered farm, or resign themselves to rainfed agriculture.

Agriculture alone cannot rescue rural areas from poverty. A broad mix of development strategies will be needed

This is particularly unfortunate in view of the fact that many white farmers have benefited handsomely from irrigation schemes sponsored by tax payers. Furthermore, water for agriculture is heavily subsidised and current tariff policies do not begin to reflect the real costs of the resource and its delivery system.

Public investment in infrastructure for agriculture has been skewed by race and politics, with the result that considerable corrective investment, or incentives to share existing infrastructure, will be needed to support equitable agricultural development. If investment in new infrastructure remains off the agenda, it is unlikely that new commercial farmers will be able to fully exploit the benefits of the new agricultural dispensation.

Conclusion

The commercial agricultural sector is undergoing a painful transition from an era of tight regulation and generous policy support to deregulation and far reaching subsidy cuts. This transition is being crosscut by new initiatives to reorient the sector's resources towards support for small scale black farmers.

Black farmers are entering the commercial sector at a time when agriculture as a whole is under severe stress, yet they will not enjoy the same protection, support and subsidies that enabled their white counterparts to establish dominance.

As individuals, black farmers who have resources of their own will be able to acquire significant agricultural holdings. However, farmers operating as groups have been able to access grants in land reform pilot areas, use the grants to leverage additional loans and thus acquire substantial agricultural holdings.

The alternative route, which has been used in a small number of cases to date, is for workers to use their grants collectively to purchase a share in an existing farming operation. By using the land reform programme resources creatively, both of these mechanisms could over time result in a significant level of black ownership of commercial agriculture.

Despite these options, it is unlikely that land reform will have much impact on the structure of the agricultural sector in the short term. The Department of Land Affairs's resources are being targeted at poverty relief, not small farmer development, and the Department of Agriculture's revised farmer support programmes presuppose land holding.

For those able to access land, whether on lease or through financed purchase, there is no assurance that they will be able to compete on equal terms with existing commercial farmers who have had decades to secure a niche and will continue to enjoy diminished, but ongoing, subsidies for some years. Limited access to water particularly will constrain the output of many.

Finally, it should be noted that however structured, agriculture alone cannot rescue South Africa's rural areas from poverty. A far broader mix of development strategies – including enterprise development, stimulation of small town economies and appropriate training – will be needed to meet the objectives of job creation and growth currently assigned to agriculture alone.

CHAPTER TEN

RESOURCE MANAGEMENT

This chapter does not directly represent findings from the Land Reform Research Programme, because natural resource management was not included in the terms of reference of the research teams. However, work on natural resource management was previously commissioned by the LAPC, and conducted during 1993 and 1994 in several parts of South Africa. That material forms the basis of this chapter.

The key to sustainable natural resource management is to integrate marginalised rural people into the formal economy

The studies included a number of overviews or 'topical' papers on water, use of arable and non-arable land, nature conservation, forestry and legal issues. They were supported by several zonal studies in conditions ranging from rural wet and semi-arid to peri-urban and industrialised rural areas.

The zonal studies involved participatory research with different land users in South Africa and former homeland situations: the Bulwer and Midlands regions of KwaZulu-Natal, the Fish River in the Eastern Cape, Citrusdal in the Western Cape, the Oliphants River in Northern Province and the Nkomazi region of Mpumalanga.

The notion of natural resource management is intrinsically linked to rural development, because the allocation of resources is important in generating sustainable livelihoods. Without access to resources there cannot be rural development, and without infrastructural support the productive potential of resources cannot be realised.

The key to sustainable natural resource management in South Africa is how best to integrate into the formal economy people from the former homelands, 'black spot' areas, labour tenants and other marginalised rural groups previously denied any basis for generating a living.

The LAPC's natural resource management studies tried to understand how economic and political policy, institutional settings and legal regimes fostered artificial resource scarcity and practices that led to resource degradation. They also tried to correlate findings on policy impacts and institutional practice in both 'white' and 'black' rural South Africa.

In addition, the studies tried to identify the main utilisation patterns in commercial and communal areas. Utilisation patterns result from various economic or cultural needs, and it is important to understand them when trying to develop appropriate mechanisms and incentives for natural resource management systems.

Natural resource management is an important aspect of the land reform programme for several reasons.

Firstly, it tries to address the problem of resource scarcity by making more resources available to more people. This is crucial, since most rural areas in the former homelands have high population densities and severe soil and water degradation. Land reform could help ease the pressure on over utilised resources by reducing population pressure and intensifying resource use.

Secondly, management is needed to provide infrastructural support through state investment in extension services, the provision of basic amenities and human resource development. These measures could help raise income levels and encourage investment in protecting the resource base.

> There needs to be equity in the allocation of resources and support mechanisms which encourage people to use their resources sustainably

Thirdly, legal and institutional reforms granting ownership over land will encourage people to protect their resources. People will utilise resources wisely as the benefits from the resource will be direct and immediate. Improvements in women's rights to natural resources is particularly crucial to any future natural resource management strategy: about 80% of resource use and management in rural areas involves women.

In general, the policy environment needs to focus less on the status of the resource and more on the causes of poor natural resource management, which can largely be attributed to inadequate incentive mechanisms created by negative social and political factors.

While in some people's minds protecting resources means keeping people off land, the long term solution lies in ensuring that there is equity in the allocation of resources and that support mechanisms are in place which encourage people to use their resources sustainably.

Often, micro-variations within broad agro-climatic conditions present the possibility for a mix of land use options in a given area

Geo-physical factors

South Africa has a number of climatic and ecological zones resulting in tremendous variations in conditions: from semi-desert to bushveld and sub-tropical.

The climate ranges from Mediterranean with winter rainfall in the Western Cape to summer rainfall for most parts of the country and sub-tropical summer rainfall along the east coast. South Africa is plagued by regular drought and on the whole is a dry country.

The topography is dominated by the Great African Plateau, which rises a short distance from the southern coastline, and in parts of the country undermines otherwise favourable climatic factors. KwaZulu-Natal, for example, has more than enough water but steepness of terrain combined with high rainfall often results in high levels of erosion.

The Cape mountains form a barrier to rainfall in the interior Karoo, but act as catchment and river systems for the fertile coastal strip. In the Eastern Cape, most of the land is moderately (53%) sloping and level land is rare. Most arable land is on slopes, which limits the size and effective use of cultivated fields.

The geo-physical conditions have implications for the kind of agriculture and land use options employed and – given the fragility of vegetation and soils and the uncertainties of water supply – for appropriate options for sustainable land use. Often, micro-variations within broad agro-climatic conditions present the possibility for a mix of land use options in a given area.

Land resources

It is estimated that about 16 million hectares of land is arable: about 13 million hectares in commercial farming areas and 2,5 million hectares in small scale farming areas of the former homelands. Non-arable land is used for extensive farming and is dominated by commercial ranching, communal grazing land under tribal authorities and nature conservation.

Livestock ownership

Livestock ownership is an integral part of Cape Nguni culture, and the people in Tyefu Location in the Fish River area are no exception. White farmers in the area are engaged in livestock ownership for more transparently commercial reasons.

It is worth noting that more than 90% of livestock in communal areas is owned by 22% of the people. This means there are wide disparities in livestock holdings, and this influences the management of rangeland resources. Most of the livestock units in Tyefu are used for domestic purposes such as milk, ritual ceremonies and meat, rather than for strictly commercial purposes.

As is the case in other communal areas, livestock is a form of investment and insurance. It is seen as a communal asset even by those who do not own stock, because they might derive direct benefit through, for instance, the slaughter of livestock for ritual ceremonies. Livestock also plays an important role as a store of wealth for the education of children, and is often sold for investment in education.

On commercial white owned farms almost 80% of the livestock are Angora goats and 5% are cattle, whereas 73% of livestock in the communal areas are cattle and the remaining 27% are sheep or indigenous goats.

Not surprisingly, indigenous breeds of cattle are generally more suited to local conditions and outperform European breeds if the total cost of production is considered. Many people in the area have nevertheless been convinced by successive Department of Agriculture extension officers to invest in European breeds such as Bonsmara.

The fact that three out of four cattle in the communal areas die of hunger or disease before reaching the market, reflects as much on the lack of markets and available agricultural extension services as it does on the propensity of people to hold onto their cattle, in the hope that drought will be broken.

It is estimated that 16 million hectares of land is arable: about 13 million in commercial farming areas and 2,5 million in the former homelands

About 60% of South Africa's soils have a low organic matter content. This makes the soil highly susceptible to erosion if it is used intensively. In the former homelands, land that is not used for crop or timber production is over stocked in communal and privately owned farming areas. Often there is under utilisation of arable land, which is overstocked with cattle because of persistent pastoralism in changing social conditions.

"While the immediate cause of degradation is too many animals, the underlying cause is too little land for the number of

people and livestock in the area east of the Fish River. The problem is compounded." (Ainslee, Fox and Fabricius 1995).

Often there is under utilisation of arable land, which is over stocked with cattle because of persistent pastoralism in changing social conditions

The effect of soil degradation is made greater off-site than on-site by the degradation of water resources through increased sedimentation, siltation and eutrophication caused largely by commercial crop and range farming (McKenzie 1994).

McKenzie argues that investment in soil conservation is not viable for farmers earning average or less than average national returns – and not many more than half of farmers earn larger than average returns.

Land used for nature conservation has been viewed by rural communities as 'havens for the rich'. Meanwhile, surrounding villages have limited land for grazing, natural woodland has been denuded to meet increasing fuel demands, and fenced off parks have denied people access to water, sources of traditional medicine and craft material.

Parks have experienced tense relations with neighbouring communities, who increasingly question the importance of protected areas when there are demands for resources. Many parks now need to address poverty and find ways of integrating growing eco-tourism with rural development objectives.

For example, the Fish River zonal study revealed that communities neighbouring the Double Drift, Andries Vosloo and Sam Knott Game Reserves have formed forums to negotiate with park authorities on how best to manage community needs to access resources in the parks.

Rights and interests

Entitlements are the most common way of allocating scarce resources. The rules deciding who has the right to access and use a resource – and how it may be used – are laid down by an authority, which may be custom and practice, a ruler, conqueror or legitimate elected legislature.

In pre-colonial times a number of customary and tribal systems regulated access to land and use of natural resources. In post-colonial South Africa, the regulation of rights to land, water, minerals and other resources became an important means for advancing the interests of certain groups in society over others.

Rewriting the rules about rights of access to land – and reallocating rights to land and other natural resources in a way which minimises potential conflicts and creates security – will be one of the most crucial aspects of land reform.

Mining rights and interests

Mining is an extremely important land use activity in South Africa, involving almost all of the nine provinces. A mining right includes the right to prospect and exploit land for minerals. In practice, mining rights supersede even private ownership, and it is not necessary for a holder of a mine right to own the land.

For example, De Beers owns the mining rights of nearly 30% of Namaqualand. It can effectively exclude other users from the land, even that which it does not mine but uses to graze substantial herds of goats and sheep. In Namaqualand Coloured Rural Areas, successive colonial administrations have consistently withheld or undermined the mineral rights of 'reserve' inhabitants (Surplus People Project 1995).

The whole of the Northern Cape is well endowed with a range of mineral deposits. However, many of the mining sectors are in sharp decline. Major diamond mines face closure early next century, while copper, lead and zinc mines have a lifespan of no more than 20 years. Other sectors such as iron ore and manganese have expected lives of between 50 to 100 years (Northern Cape Synthesis Report 1995).

The allocation of mining rights to a few results in mining profits not remaining in the areas where minerals are found. Mineral laws and the allocation of mineral rights should be reformed to allow benefits to flow to local communities. Low cost and low technology exploitation of mineral resources also needs to be explored, with the aim of energising otherwise inhospitable regions.

Mining 'interests' refer to the vested interests pursuing the exploitation of mineral resources without interference and disturbance, and using other natural resources – such as water and land – in the process. These interests need to be weighed up against the interests of other land users who may want land for, among other things, an undisturbed natural environment, or for farming, recreation or residential purposes.

Rewriting the rules about rights of access to land will be one of the most crucial aspects of land reform

Water resources

Land without access to water resources will pose many challenges to rural development. There are several reasons for water scarcity in South Africa, ranging from climatic conditions to patterns of allocation and distribution fostered by policies that favoured white agriculture, industry and domestic use.

Historically, water rights were allocated in agricultural areas, with the rights of farmers along rivers protected. However, with increasing demands from the industrial sector and the growth of towns, the 1956 Water Act was passed to ensure equitable distribution of water between competing users. These divergent interests remain, with competition increasing and relating both to water resource allocation and the development of water supplies.

The availability of water, for example, has been identified as the single greatest constraint on growth and development in Northern Province, where water supply infrastructure lags far behind the demand from a rapidly growing population. There is also conflict between the use of scarce water for rural domestic purposes and for irrigation schemes.

The availability of water has been identified as the single greatest constraint on growth and development in Northern Province

About two thirds of South Africa receives less than 500 millimetres of rainfall annually. Over the years the water requirements of agriculture – which is the main user of water – had to be supplemented from other sources, which led to the building of large dams, irrigation projects and management structures.

Western Cape water

Agriculture is the biggest consumer of water in the Western Cape. But the greater Cape Town metropolitan area, which relies on the same water supply sources, is placing increasing demands on water supply in the province. Already a substantial proportion of the Western Cape's population – 69% – is located in Cape Town.

Furthermore, irrigated agriculture – most agriculture in the Western Cape – has a tremendous impact on the environment, water particularly. Irrigation leads to an increase in the salt content of rivers, as research in the Breede River area during the last two decades suggests, and causes severe environmental deterioration and soil damage (Moolman 1995, unpublished draft).

These policies led to many villages being displaced to remote areas, permanently alienating them from their main source of livelihood. In some cases, ill conceived needs led to large scale irrigation schemes in the homelands when there were other more pressing needs. The Tyefu irrigation scheme in Fish River is a case in point: the demand for water seems to be mostly to meet domestic needs.

Commercial farmers have also been blamed for indiscriminate use of fertilisers and pesticides. That and the discharging of polluted water by industry are major sources of concern to rural communities.

While subsidised irrigation schemes and other benefits were being introduced for white commercial farmers, a similar level of investment in the former homelands was strikingly absent. And with the monopolisation of watersheds or upper catchment areas by commercial agriculture and forestry, rural communities living downstream suffer a poor supply of water, in terms of quality and quantity.

Bad water practices

Present levels of water use in the Citrusdal Irrigation Board area are unsustainable. To some extent, this is reflected downstream of the Clanwilliam Dam, where demand exceeds supply.

Existing allocations and practices, such as the construction of private dams and uncontrolled use of private water, reflect neither the availability of water nor the ecosystem needs of the river. The lack of available information on levels of nutrient inputs and pesticide contamination in the upper Olifants River catchment is preventing proactive management.

Although water scarcity has compelled the use of more efficient irrigation systems, there is a lack of control over abstraction and few incentives exist to conserve water. There is thus considerable scope to improve the efficiency of water use.

The legislative and administrative framework governing water use in the Olifants River catchment area is inequitable, placing upstream and private water users in a preferential situation. This results in considerable conflict between farmers during low flow periods. Water restrictions disadvantage farmers who have not developed to the same extent as others.

Water restrictions disadvantage farmers who have not developed to the same extent as others

In poorer areas of South Africa, domestic demand for water is increasing: it appears to be the main priority, followed by subsistence agriculture and livestock production. Stark disparities in water allocation were illustrated in one of the case studies.

In the Nkomazi area of Kangwane, the Driekoppies Dam – which sources its water from the Lomati River – adequately serves the needs of sugar cane farmers and communities in the Driekoppies dam area, while communities in the neighbouring Boschfontein and Madadeni areas have no secure water provision, relying on water to be delivered in tanks or illegally tapping water from irrigation pipes.

The key policy issue to reconcile is the conflict between land as a productive commodity and land for social purposes

The Boschfontein and Madadeni communities tend to pay more per litre than the commercial farmers, who enjoy the support and services of irrigation boards. The irregular supply of water to poor rural households also limits their use of their land. Competition between poor rural households, commercial agriculture and other users will increase and become a potential source of conflict.

In other areas, like Mpumalanga and KwaZulu-Natal, water scarcity has been blamed on extensive afforestation in the main catchment areas. The forests are mostly in recharge zones, and with proper planning and better management the flow of water could be increased from catchment sites. Some reduction in water flow has been attributed to invasions by exotic species like black wattle.

In periods of drought, white commercial farmers relied extensively on groundwater while poor rural communities suffered drastic reductions in water supply.

Existing rights to water in South Africa are disproportionate, with about 60% of water held in private hands. The system of riparian rights – which individuals acquire through land ownership – entitles land owners to use water for domestic purposes, irrigation and watering livestock. Water legislation and administrative systems have not adequately addressed the problems of those who do not hold riparian rights (Bromley 1995).

Conclusion

The findings of the land reform programme have several implications. Competition over land and resource use and allocation is a critical aspect of any land reform programme. Given that significant demand for land for residential purposes was reported in all provinces, the competition between land for settlement and land for other uses will need regulation.

The key policy issue to reconcile – given the pent-up demand for land resulting from overcrowding in townships and former homelands, rapid urbanisation and population growth – is the conflict between land as a productive commodity and land for social purposes.

Land reform can change settlement and demographic patterns, impacting on the kind and location of infrastructural support required to meet needs. There will continue to be demands for energy as well as for water, sanitation and related services.

If energy demands are not met through electrification in peri-urban areas and social programmes in remote areas, natural woodland will be stripped. The integration of alternative fuel sources into development plans may alleviate some energy demands.

Water provision will be influenced by changes in legislation, and investment will have to be made in setting up reticulation systems and other supply infrastructure. Water tanks to trap rain water from roofs, village dams or water pumps may meet some of the water demands of villages.

Communal grazing can be rescued from the prejudice that traditional systems have suffered by improving the tenurial system and creating legitimate authority structures to manage such systems.

Stocking densities are likely to increase if traditional value systems are revived, but densities must be regulated by increasing the use of veld through rotating pastoralism. It is important to remember that regulating stock numbers alone will not solve farmers' problems: alternative livelihoods and asset accumulations also need to be introduced.

> Incentives and support can encourage behavioural patterns and land use practice which ensures the sustainable use of natural resources

Many of our studies showed that land is not only earmarked for agricultural or livestock production: many people are also interested in non-farming activities such as eco-tourism, small crafts industries and food processing as alternative sources of income. In areas like Glenmore in Fish River, communities are investing in housing because they believe rural areas to be safer than urban centres.

Monitoring natural resource use will be important, and can be done effectively by the users of the resource themselves. One cannot legislate better management, but incentives and support such as extension services and education can encourage behavioural patterns and land use practice which ensures the sustainable use of natural resources.

CHAPTER ELEVEN

INSTITUTIONAL SUPPORT SYSTEMS

Critique is easy, but there is little yet to relieve the unease that charting the institutional landscape of rural South Africa generates. Much of the old has not yet died, and the new is far from born. The systematic neglect of the rural poor will cast a long shadow over current attempts to achieve both social justice and rural revival through land reform.

The systematic neglect of the rural poor will cast a long shadow over attempts to achieve social justice and rural revival through land reform

In many respects, rural areas have been treated as a residual category. 'People in rural areas' include labour tenants, shack dwellers in remote informal settlements, factory workers commuting daily from rural dormitory villages, taxi and spaza entrepreneurs, and unemployed youth with no interest in farming – alongside the better known categories of farmers, farm workers and aspirant farmers.

Agricultural livelihoods are incidental to many of them, and the range of their institutional needs is exceeded only by their aspirations.

Nonetheless, the main points which emerge are depressingly similar – a vast institutional infrastructure which has virtually ignored the rural majority: uneven popular organisation; few non-governmental organisations with the skills and capacity to support rural restructuring initiatives; limited private sector involvement outside the well resourced commercial agriculture sector; misdirected spending; and, well into the New South Africa, poor coordination among those agencies able to transform the rural hinterland.

What institutions are needed?

The responses of informants around the country underline the point that people on the ground understand land reform as infinitely wider than mere land transfers.

The first demand of most people is for secure residential land – with services. Safe and reliable drinking water, transport services to help them access jobs, towns and amenities, schools, health care, electricity: these basic needs rate far higher than the agricultural support mechanisms prioritised by conventional wisdom.

Clearly there is a great need for access to credit, agricultural inputs and markets: no small farmer initiative can succeed for long without them. But for the majority of beneficiaries under the land reform programme, they will be secondary needs.

The implications of this emphasis on basic servicing are profound. Proposals to extend irrigation schemes and open up irrigable land to small scale farmers, for example, are questionable when considered against the need of the majority for safe drinking water.

More importantly, perhaps, if resources are diverted from impoverished and under serviced rural areas to drive high profile projects, the ensuing resentment from those left on the sidelines will seriously undermine any prospect of sustainable change.

The institutional framework for services to support the land reform programme will have to be grafted onto existing local authority systems and organisational networks to ensure that decisions implemented locally respond to, and address local needs. Yet the appropriate institutional skeleton barely exists at local level.

Traditional authority structures have been grossly distorted by the ambitions of previous governments and are not equipped to address the new challenges of rural governance. They co-exist uneasily alongside emergent forms of local organisation and representation.

Many farm workers live in small island settlements on white farms, where the farmer himself personifies local government.

> The institutional framework for services to support land reform will have to be grafted onto existing systems

Hundreds of thousands of people in South Africa's rural areas live in sprawling informal settlements, akin to those on the urban periphery except for the complete absence of local jobs and services. There are no local authorities there to direct local development, and a negligible local tax base to pay for it.

The grinding poverty of most rural areas means the ability of local residents to pay for services is very limited. Given that grant aid and RDP funding is finite, the Government cannot afford less than full cost recovery on service delivery. Inevitably, it seems likely that it will be some time before the tangible benefits of the new South Africa are evident in poor areas.

> The third tier of government simply does not exist effectively in most parts of the country

Infrastructural development and service delivery falls within the jurisdiction of local government, working in conjunction with the RDP. In large areas of the country though, there is currently little capacity at local level to undertake the coordination, administration and financial management necessary to drive local infrastructural development.

Third tier government simply does not exist effectively in most parts of the country: the focus of legislation and transformative energy has been urban areas. It would have been naive to imagine that the mere establishment of new structures of rural local government after democratic local elections would make an immediate difference.

The undefined legal framework of pre-election rural local government structures resulted in a number of local institutions, like civics, taking on local government functions and forming negotiating forums. They were not catered for by law, and attempts to transform negotiating forums into Transitional Local Councils had very mixed results (Eastern Cape Synthesis report 1995).

Conflicts have been particularly pronounced where *amakhosi*, traditional authorities and civics have had different perceptions of what constitutes democratic local government.

There has been minimal coordination between official structures, local offices of line ministries, regional services councils and residual provincial administrations.

What rural areas do have, however, is the infinite resourcefulness of people who have weathered the neglect of bureaucrats and official structures.

Broadly speaking, participants in the land reform programme will need institutional support and servicing in three areas: local government, agricultural development, and rural entrepreneurial development.

The difficulties of transforming existing institutions to meet these needs should not be underestimated, given that they were established to meet fundamentally different objectives. All too often they have become organs for the delivery of patronage, not services.

Infrastructure and service delivery

❒ Rural local government

Central government has designated local government as the primary implementing agency of the RDP in rural areas, given the virtual absence of other statutory bodies outside urban settlements. Certainly, local decision making will be imperative to effectively tailor the limited resources of the RDP to best support local development initiatives.

Centralised bureaucracies, of necessity, operate at the level of generalised policies which cannot anticipate the needs and concerns of diverse settlements and communities. Experience the world over confirms that bureaucracies tend to be inflexible, unimaginative and largely inaccessible to the majority of rural people.

Given the importance of local decision making, it is discomforting to note that local capacity to engage in development planning and project implementation is poorly developed at present, especially in rural areas.

Compared to the relatively well funded and experienced urban local authorities, rural local government will operate at a great disadvantage, both in terms of human and material resources. There are simply not enough skilled personnel available to ensure cost effective and efficient service delivery nationwide.

A tension is inevitable between political pressure for swift and efficient upgrading of services and infrastructure, and equally strong political pressure for locally controlled implementation.

> What rural areas do have is the infinite resourcefulness of people who have weathered neglect

In former 'white areas', local government was well established through autonomous local government entities in larger towns, and through local authority councils in very small towns. There were no formal representative structures for white rural areas, although white farmers were represented indirectly on the Regional Services Councils (RSCs) or Joint Services Boards (JSBs).

The RSCs were established from the mid-1980s to facilitate development by redistributing income and channelling funds to capital projects. From the early 1990s, the Councils also started delivering bulk services in some areas, like water and electricity, and emergency services like fire protection and ambulances.

There was no comparable provision for local government in the former bantustans, where the RSCs had no jurisdiction and thus did not fund capital projects or support servicing.

> In terms of representation, there are widely divergent traditions, practices and levels of popular participation

Traditional authorities were expected to manage local services, but very few had the capacity or resources to do this. Local government services in rural areas were provided by second tier bantustan government departments working in conjunction with traditional authority structures.

Coordination was generally poor, and the combination of under funding and poorly trained, unmotivated and unaccountable staff left an endowment of infrastructural decay. Service delivery in fact deteriorated after April 1994 in many areas, as key sub-regional personnel were transferred to provincial capitals.

Given the range of structures that need to be harmonised, transforming rural local government will be extremely complex and challenging. On the service delivery side, there are extreme disparities in experience, resources, funding, staffing and capacity. In terms of representation, there are widely divergent traditions, practices and levels of popular participation.

There are political structures even in the most remote areas of the country – tribal councils, civics and village committees of various kinds – even if they cannot claim to represent all local interests adequately or democratically. Their ability to effect service delivery varies from adequate to almost non-existent.

The low credibility of formal representative structures before 1994 legitimised the range of popular structures which emerged alongside statutory bodies. This process continued after the general elections, with a range of new bodies forming – local RDP committees, development forums and committees, their satellite structures and so on.

Institutional confusion was exacerbated by lack of clarity about how rural local government would function. Registration of voters for local elections proceeded in the absence of any clarity on the role, function and resources the new structures would exploit.

New rural local government structures were established in most provinces in November 1995. Many aspects of their role and function remain undefined. Often, the new councils co-exist uneasily alongside pre-existing development and tribal authority structures, and power struggles are being played out for control of local resources and decision making

The new councils may have primacy at a formal level: in practice, very often they lack the experience or credibility to take over functions performed well by older structures which are regarded by many as equally valid and representative.

Parallel structures, lack of clarity over fiscal transfer arrangements and major deficiencies in capacity in rural local structures could impact badly on rural development initiatives, and slow down the delivery of support services and infrastructure which the beneficiaries of the land reform programme will require.

Particular constituencies in rural areas may fare better than others in accessing institutions and the resources they offer. Farm workers face continued marginalisation unless concerted efforts are made to include them in public debates and representative structures. Many are physically isolated on large commercial farms, inhibiting effective local organisation and information flows.

Women have particularly pressing needs which are not necessarily prioritised by local organisations dominated by men. Generally, women headed households are the poorest, and women are most affected by lack of services and housing.

Across the country, it is clear that most rural women remain outside the political process and do not participate much in local organisations or development committees. The district studies highlight the fact that women have less access to public information than men, and consequently are at a disadvantage in pressing their claims for subsidies, services and support.

> As long as women do not participate actively in decision making, it is unlikely their development needs will be met

As long as women are not represented, and do not participate actively in decision making structures, it is unlikely that their development needs will be met (Eastern Cape District Study 1995).

❐ Traditional authorities

Traditional leaders in many areas are under pressure both from the Government and rural villagers to cede many of the powers they accumulated during the apartheid years. They face a particular challenge from people testing customary land tenure and matrimonial practices which discriminate against women's access to land.

This growing pressure could prompt a backlash, particularly in the Eastern Cape and KwaZulu-Natal, with chiefs holding strongly onto powers they currently enjoy. Control over land allocation is one issue they mobilise around. This, combined with a possible reassertion of masculinist customs and values, could further prejudice women's access to land and resources.

Traditional leaders in many areas are under pressure to cede many of the powers they accumulated during apartheid

All chiefs were allocated seats *ex officio* on transitional rural local councils – in part to assign them a formal place in the new structure of local government, and partly to ensure they did not contest the local elections for full membership of the council, lest this split communities.

But tension between the role and functions of the chieftaincy, local government and local development structures is likely to persist for some time, not least because rural people in many parts of the country where the chieftaincy retains credibility seem to be in little doubt that chiefs will continue to control land allocations, demand tribal levies and influence local decision making through the tribal council.

It seems tribal councils will remain operative in many areas, because people are accustomed to them and many accept their authority. New rural local government structures may well be established parallel to them, but in many areas it seems tribal councils will remain the real seat of local decision making (Eales 1995).

❐ District councils

An elaborate mesh of district and sub-regional structures is being developed around the country to bridge the gap between provincial and local government, and to address the twin problems of limited capacity and inadequate revenue bases to fund local servicing.

The former Regional Services Councils and Joint Services Boards in KwaZulu-Natal are playing a key role, and their areas of jurisdiction have been vastly expanded.

The Northern Province RSC, for example, previously spanned several magisterial districts in former 'white' Transvaal. Renamed the Northern Services Council, it now encompasses all of what used to be Venda and large portions of Gazankulu and Lebowa. It will be entirely responsible for services rendered at local level by the former bantustan governments, and will function as an interim local government agency, undertaking service delivery and maintaining infrastructure wherever cost effective and necessary.

For the next few years at least, the services councils' funding will come from provincial governments, primarily through RDP grants. Because of their dependence on regional government for finance, it seems inevitable that the councils will be answerable to regional government in the first instance, rather than to emerging local government structures (McIntosh 1994).

There is no shortage of personnel to undertake services: the problem lies in finding sufficient competent and motivated staff with the managerial skills required to ensure that services like electricity and water are extended to areas that need them.

The same pool of public servants who presided over rural service delivery under the previous regime now staff regional, district and local offices of the new administrations.

There is a very real chance that the most capable staff members will be concentrated at head office, as there is a widespread perception in most bureaucracies that rural areas are backwaters, beneath the dignity of competent and ambitious officials. The presence of less than dynamic staff members at local and district level could constrain effective service delivery, and bolster the trend towards provincial centralism.

❒ Provincial government

Re-integrating each province administratively and forging a coherent and productive civil service is the priority of the provincial governments. Unfortunately for politicians mandated to deliver swiftly on the RDP, the task of administrative restructuring is vast, cumbersome and almost invisible to their constituents.

The same pool of public servants who presided over rural service delivery under the previous regime now staff the new administrations

With the exception of the Western and Northern Cape, where there were no bantustans, all of the provinces are having to address acute administrative fragmentation and duplication. Until the new provincial governments have asserted their authority decisively over their vast bureaucracies – there are 120 000 civil servants in KwaZulu-Natal and 156 000 in Northern Province – they have little room to manoeuvre.

The administrative problems facing provincial governments cannot be under estimated. They inherited an inefficient, bloated and fragmented array of institutions, which had little experience of accountable service delivery or bottom up development initiatives.

Provincial government departments have the capacity to make or break land reform initiatives in their regions

Also, provincial governments have had no alternative but to centralise their bureaucracies wherever possible to achieve integration: thus, regional unity and coherence will almost certainly be attained at the cost of nurturing local capacity and local autonomy.

Unless regional governments actively help new local government and development bodies to make their own decisions about how resources are allocated and managed locally, it is likely that most decisions about how rural restructuring is defined and implemented will be made in provincial capitals by people who do not have all the information on local conditions they need.

Clearly, there is an urgent need for mediating structures like NGOs and private sector agencies to help bridge this information and capacity gap.

The provincial restructuring process is drawing on at least three institutional bases – provincial, bantustan and central government – which are structurally and culturally different, geographically fragmented and designed to achieve fundamentally different objectives to those now required (Forsyth 1994).

At times the establishment of functional departments is complicated by tensions between central and provincial government. The Western Cape and KwaZulu-Natal provincial legislatures are not led by the ANC, and may prove reluctant to implement to the letter what they regard as ANC policies. Even in ANC led provincial legislatures, there is not always complete harmony between regional and central government land reform policy frameworks.

Provincial government departments have the capacity to make or break land reform initiatives in their regions. Much can be achieved where provincial governments provide their officials with the resources and latitude to address the task at hand: rapid progress being achieved in the preparatory stages of the land pilot programmes in Mpumalanga and the Free State illustrates the point very well.

On the down side, there is much room for grandstanding, as in KwaZulu-Natal, where the national Department of Land Affairs is dependent on the active cooperation of the provincial departments of agriculture, traditional affairs and local government.

There are clear signs that the provincial departments regard the central government's land reform initiative as high handed and inadequately consultative. As KwaZulu-Natal has the single largest provincial population and some of the most acute indicators of rural poverty, the province is the loser in the stand off.

Tensions between central and provincial governments are also emerging in other areas, with key central government departments such as Land Affairs, and Water Affairs and Forestry, being the butt of regional resentments.

The land reform programme is being coordinated by the national Department of Land Affairs and administered by provincial land affairs officials and sub-committees, working – to a greater or lesser degree – with relevant provincial departments such as agriculture, housing and local government, and RDP structures.

Land Affairs has minimal implementation capacity, as currently structured, and is thus reliant on remote structures over which it has little control. Sound coordination and clear communication will be essential to ensure that the whole process does not bog down in a welter of committees which decide little and can implement nothing.

Already problems are developing between regional RDP structures, provincial line function departments responsible for land reform, and the Department of Land Affairs in some provinces over the boundaries of jurisdiction for different aspects of the pilot land reform programme. All it takes is a little officiousness or procedural insensitivity at committee level for pilot programmes to be set back several months.

There are problems between RDP structures, provincial departments and the Department of Land Affairs in some provinces

Pressure to show progress in achieving national objectives is generating tensions around water infrastructure development. A conflict developed rapidly between the central Department of Water Affairs and the KwaZulu-Natal government on precisely this issue.

Water resource management is a national competency, and Water Affairs is reorienting itself away from a focus on dam building and macro-management towards a greater emphasis on supplying water to people – especially in rural areas.

Conflicts with regional institutions have emerged as the Directorate moves into water supply on the ground in some areas and engages directly with local consumers, completely bypassing structures like the regional department of agriculture and rural development agencies (Sapsford 1995).

Aside from turf battles and institutional conflicts, an important variable in implementing a viable land reform programme is the capacity of regional governments to spend funds allocated to them timeously and well.

It is widely assumed that the Government and its agencies are the best vehicles for implementing development

The central government's RDP commission is working closely with the Department of Land Affairs to support the pilot land reform initiative, and funds are being disbursed by the Commission to the provincial government department mandated to implement the programme. But this process is going much more slowly than anticipated, for a range of reasons.

In many parts of the country, provincial RDP commissions have experienced difficulty in consolidating their linkages with rural development initiatives. Communication, cooperation and coordination with existing development forums is very limited, and the RDP structures have not yet developed either the capacity or the institutions needed to 'deliver development' on their own.

The non-governmental sector

Recent research shows a widespread tendency among South Africans to assume that the state will – unasked – provide the services needed to establish and sustain a viable land reform programme.

Expectations of the new Government are such that district studies in several parts of the country reported a decline in some local organisations and development structures – like water committees – after the April 1994 elections, as a result of the assumption that they were no longer necessary now that the new Government was in place to address people's needs (Murray 1995a).

Moreover, it is widely assumed that the Government and its agencies are the most appropriate vehicles for implementing development projects and policies. This is often not the case, particularly where the public sector does not yet have the skills and experience to support local development initiatives.

There is growing evidence in South Africa of grassroots initiatives in which representatives of rural settlements, supported by NGOs, design projects and negotiate the funds they require from donors.

Rural water supply projects funded by the Mvula Trust exemplify this in the Eastern Cape, KwaZulu-Natal, Mpumalanga and Northern Province. Mvula Trust is an NGO which is commissioning and overseeing the implementation of infrastructural projects on behalf of a government department, in this case the Department of Water Affairs.

NGOs and private sector agencies capable of providing technical support and training in rural areas are in critically short supply. Yet there has been little apparent questioning in government of what activities and responsibilities pertinent to rural servicing and development should be passed over to NGOs, the private sector and community based bodies, or what incentives or assistance they will need to encourage them to assume new roles.

Indeed, all too often the incentives are negative. New government structures in some parts of the country have shown little interest in working jointly with NGOs, perhaps for fear of showing up their own lack of experience in rural development.

More concretely, slow payment – or even no payment at all – for work undertaken on behalf of the public sector is a powerful disincentive to effective partnerships with non-governmental agencies.

It must be acknowledged that the NGO sector is not buoyant in South Africa at present. Cutbacks in donor funding, poor relations with regional government in some provinces, loss of key staff to Parliament and the public service, and internal disputes have all served to reduce their effectiveness.

> There is a critical shortage of NGOs and private sector agencies capable of providing support and training in rural areas

Beyond the core affiliates of the National Land Committee, few NGOs have invested time in exploring land reform policy debates and most are simply not equipped to advise communities on best courses of action.

Many NGOs are grappling with how to redefine their identity in the new South Africa. For NGOs which have long seen their role as including political opposition and criticism, to begin collaborating with government in joint programmes and implementing elements of public programmes, implies a profound change in identity (Farrington *et al* 1993).

There is also understandable resentment towards government among some NGOs because many funders now assign grant and development finances directly to the public sector. For their part, there is no reason why democratic governments should look favourably on NGOs, whose very existence implies a criticism of the government's shortcomings (Farrington *et al* 1994).

NGOs are able to reach marginalised communities and strengthen local capacity more effectively than government

Nevertheless, NGOs have an extremely valuable contribution to make to the land reform programme. They are able to reach marginalised communities more effectively than government structures, and increasing numbers of them are adept at strengthening local capacity to manage development initiatives.

There is a need for the Government to involve NGOs more closely in the land reform process than it does at present. Government needs to identify complementary roles for certain NGOs and, where necessary, support should be provided to NGO staff to enable them to fulfil these roles.

NGOs, for example, are extremely well placed to advise regional planning committees on local dynamics, capacities and infrastructural bottlenecks, and their extensive experience in organisational development, training and policy support fills a gap which government will not have the capacity to address for years to come. NGOs and private sector agents do not incur recurrent costs for government, so channelling programmes through them will not incur increases in public expenditure.

At the very least there is a need for better communication and coordination between government and the NGO sector, so that the resources of both can complement each other. On a more practical note, uncoordinated activities can lead to misallocation of scarce resources, replication of mistakes, conflicting approaches and inappropriate decisions which backfire on the rural poor.

A classic example of the latter is the donation of borehole water pumps to a remote rural settlement. These were non-standard pumps which required imported spares, and the local works department was left responsible for maintenance.

Community based organisations

Probably the single most important local institution in many rural settlements is the Church, with its promise of spiritual, moral, socio-economic and welfare support. Dominant church figures frequently hold positions of authority in secular organisations.

A wide range of organisations exist at local level – from burial societies and *stokvels* to civic associations, advice offices, political parties and development forums. Most are not particularly strong, competent or representative, and the incidence of internal division is high.

It is highly unlikely that many currently have the capacity to undertake the local planning, organisation and implementation of district land reform initiatives, particularly where conflicts over land rights and resources could rip communities apart.

Civics exist in virtually every settlement, and are widely acknowledged as being important in promoting development. In many areas civics have played a valuable role in involving local people in community initiatives and development projects. However, they are dominated by men and the social strata from which the leaders are drawn.

Across the country, it seems that most rural woman remain outside the political process and do not participate much in community based organisations or development committees.

Women's activism tends to focus on local self help associations, like the Care Groups of Northern Province, which engage in health education and activities such as soap and fence making, community gardens and water tanks for their gardens. Community garden groups are an obvious target for support and training by extension services, but have been largely ignored.

Demand led reform and institutional support

> It benefits nobody to overstate the capacities of marginalised and impoverished people. Outsiders will be crucial in assisting them

The Department of Land Affairs is adamant that land reform must be demand driven, primarily to avoid the imposition of initiatives which do not meet local needs. The Department will facilitate and subsidise the process of assisting poor people to access land, but the policy directive is clear: initiative must come from those who want the land.

Yet in the platteland and deep rural areas of the country, there is a widespread belief among rural people that their land needs are self evident, and that they need to do nothing more than wait for land redistribution agents to find them.

This raises important questions about the capacity of the 'poorest of the poor' to organise themselves to access government support and resources, and to demonstrate the 'demand' stipulated by the Government's demand driven land reform programme.

It benefits nobody to overstate the capacities of impoverished and marginalised people. Evidence from the contemporary international literature suggests that the very poor do not organise themselves, and that poverty and high risk livelihoods are two of the most significant obstacles to popular participation in membership organisations (Farrington *et al* 1993).

Conversely, there are groups who are extremely well organised to articulate their demands, notably commercial farmers, traditional authorities and rural communities who have had extensive contact with service NGOs.

Outsiders will be crucial in assisting marginalised people to address their identified needs. Training support, and capacity building in particular, will be critical. NGOs are probably best placed to address this, perhaps in conjunction with central and regional government departments and the private sector.

Responding to the land and servicing needs of the rural poor presupposes an institutional framework which can mobilise, channel and process land claims and development proposals efficiently. It is imperative that the Department of Land Affairs implements an education and information strategy to reach the people its land reform policies are aimed at.

In the absence of appropriate institutions, participation by rural people in the planning and implementation of the land reform programme will be an event rather than a process (Farrington *et al* 1993).

> The Department of Agriculture aspires to redistribute available resources more evenly among a far wider constituency of farmers

Agricultural support and services

Agricultural support services have been aimed primarily at the large scale commercial sector. A host of technical support services – from both the public and private sector – are on offer, ranging from credit facilities to research institutions, marketing support agencies, extension services and subsidy schemes.

Despite the protestations of members of the Conservative Party, the Government has not turned its back on the country's main food producers, and nor is it likely to. What the new policy directive of the Department of Agriculture does aspire to do is to redistribute available resources more evenly among a far wider constituency of farmers.

However, it is debatable whether the requirements of an innovative and sustainable rural development programme can be grafted successfully onto the existing framework of service delivery, particularly when the framework has not proved particularly effective in developing and supporting small farmers.

In the past, separate service structures were established for white commercial and bantustan farmers. As a result, the agricultural services sector is in the throes of the same process of rationalisation and integration as the rest of the country.

Officials of former bantustan departments pose a particular challenge to the rationalisation process, in view of the very low technical skills levels of most staff members: the vast majority have minimal practical farming experience and little to offer small scale and subsistence farmers (Hayward and Botha 1995; Kirsten *et al* 1995).

Considerable funds were directed towards boosting agricultural productivity in former bantustans. With some exceptions, the return on this vast investment has been poor.

In their drive to promote commercial agriculture and the use of farming systems premised on very different resource bases, bantustan agricultural service bodies largely neglected the needs of most subsistence farmers. And by encouraging small farmers to take up credit facilities before they fully appreciated the risks, credit structures introduced indebtedness and at times compromised food production through the promotion of cash crops (Carnegie, McIntosh and Vaughan 1994).

Government and non-government agencies offer a range of technical support services, but in an uncoordinated and inefficient manner

The regional research reports make it clear that government and non-government agencies offer a range of technical support services, but do so in an uncoordinated and inefficient manner, frequently parallel to each other.

There is often no clear division of responsibility between provincial departments of agriculture and restructured development corporations, for example, and both frequently offer the same services to the same client base in the same area – while ignoring the adjacent hinterland.

Retraining and redirecting the activities of extension officers to equip them to assist newly settled farmers and food gardeners may prove difficult to achieve in the short term, given the prevailing character of extension services.

While there are often excellent field staff, the bias in former 'white" farming areas has been exclusively towards commercial farmers, and in the former bantustans primarily towards 'emergent' farmers.

Providing support to small farmers will require a shift in emphasis away from commercial production, towards support for crops which require minimal inputs and can tolerate aridity and low potential soils. Extension services will also need to address the range of complementary skills which small farmers need, ranging from negotiating skills to small business management.

Helping small farmers will require a shift towards support for crops which require minimal inputs and can tolerate aridity and low potential soils

All too often, extension services have focused on addressing problems identified by bureaucrats rather than articulated by local farmers. Institutional linkages are critical to the success of extension services, so that farmers have a say over the type of services provided for them and extension officers become more accountable to their clients.

Where local structures which mediate interventions – like farmers' committees – are unrepresentative, unresponsive or torpid, local access to credit, information and technical support can be skewed badly. This is particularly true for women farmers, who seldom participate as equals in farmers' committees dominated by men.

All too often the poor stay poor, as their meagre resources do not attract the attention of extension services.

Development corporations

Despite their dubious history, former bantustan development corporations have been granted a new lease of life. New amalgamated provincial entities are being established in most provinces.

For example, in the Free State the Thaba Nchu division of Agricor and Agribank, Bophuthatswana's agricultural development corporation and agricultural bank, have been merged with QwaQwa's Highlands Conservation Corporation and Agriqwa, to form the Agricultural Development and Eco-Tourism Company.

The details of how they will coordinate their activities with provincial departments is not clear. Nor is it clear whether the restructuring will amount to anything more than a change in name.

In Northern Province particularly, development corporations acquired an extraordinary reputation for bribery, corruption and fraud. Many officials involved in corrupt practices still hold high office. Less spectacular but more damaging has been their track record of inefficiency, paternalism and arrogance.

As their staffing arrangements remain largely intact, it is debatable whether development corporations are the most appropriate institutions to support rural development.

However, in view of the weak capacity of many provincial government departments, development corporations look set to broaden their mandate considerably into the terrain of community development, alongside their previous functions of credit provision, small farmer support and enterprise development.

Funding and financial support

Government funding institutions are poorly coordinated, and it is doubtful that government structures at regional level will have the financial and institutional capacity to deliver adequate financial support services in rural areas for some time.

Establishing effective structures to ensure safe and efficient disbursement of start-up grants to land reform participants poses major logistical problems even before the thornier questions of leveraged finance and production credit are raised.

Lack of access to credit was identified repeatedly as a constraint for small farmers

Lack of access to credit was identified repeatedly in the district studies as a constraint for small farmers, both for land purchase and production. The nature of the obstacle varies, from difficulties in getting the chairperson of the local credit board – invariably the local magistrate – to agree to visit the small farmer's land to vet the application *in situ*, to difficulties in providing acceptable collateral.

The focus of rural financial support at present is the established agricultural commercial sector: no provision whatsoever exists for micro and occasional surplus producers, and financial assistance and after care for small farmers is sparse.

The Land and Agricultural Bank and the former bantustan agricultural banks serve only commercial farmers at present. Several commercial banks are now developing products targeted at viable emergent farmers on freehold land, coupled with financial management training, and are piloting them in several areas.

There is a pressing need for more local markets and improved access to larger, more distant outlets

Providing loan finance to micro-farmers poses particular difficulties to financiers. The banking sector in South Africa has had little experience in assessing development risk, and lacks the staff to deal with large scale land and rural financing at community level.

As a sector, small farmers have had minimal exposure to conventional banking practices and can offer little in the way of conventional collateral.

In view of this, it is encouraging to note that the Strauss Commission of Inquiry into Rural Financial Services is investigating alternative forms of security, like livestock, and collateral substitutes like peer pressure, to secure small loans.

The Commission is also exploring the possibility of partnerships between NGOs, community based organisations and commercial banks to help poor borrowers access credit for land purchases and production.

Markets

Bad roads, distance from markets, transport logistics and the high cost of moving goods discourage many small farmers from trying to market surpluses. Instead, they tend to produce only what they can consume themselves and sell locally.

As the success of all agriculture beyond the purely subsistence level is crucially dependent on access to markets, there is a pressing need for more local markets and improved access to larger, more distant outlets. Periodic markets – explained later – may provide a partial answer in remote areas.

Even close proximity to a produce market does not necessarily ensure access. Several black farmers in the Messina area of the Northern Province claim they have been discriminated against on racial grounds by marketing agents, and that only those well connected to former bantustan governments – or able to buy their way in – can access produce markets.

Agricultural training

South Africa is well provided with agricultural training centres. Almost without exception, they are geared to prepare students for high tech, high input, high risk commercial farming in well watered zones rather than subsistence production in marginal soils under arid conditions.

LAPC researchers found no centres offering aftercare and ongoing support to former students: this appears to be the responsibility of the extension services.

There is, however, a growing appreciation in training facilities of the need to address the concerns of small scale and subsistence farmers, although appropriate environmental management does not seem to be particularly high on the training agenda, except in the most rudimentary sense.

Several reports noted that although the skills levels of farm workers are frequently fairly high, they do not necessarily have the skills required for small scale, low input farming.

New initiatives

It is true that South Africa has no significant track record of successful support programmes aimed at subsistence and small scale farmers, and limited experience in assisting rural enterprise initiatives. Yet there are very positive signs that many institutions are attempting to redirect their activities to address the needs of small farmers.

> There are signs that many institutions are attempting to redirect their activities to address the needs of small farmers

Some of the large grain cooperatives – decisive earlier this century in stifling the emergence of black commercial farmers – are now recruiting black members. In the Free State, for example, a number of black commercial farmers from former QwaQwa belong to the powerful Sentraal-Oos cooperative, and market their surplus grain through it.

Others are willing to help establish small farmers on the land and provide technical support in the form of soil testing, farm planning, farmer training and so on.

In the Northern Cape and Western Cape, powerful agri-business interests like Unifruco are behind a new small farmer development agency, the Small Farmers Development Corporation, which aims to mobilise and lend finance and provide technical support. The Farmer Foundation has initiated the concept of franchised small farmer support agencies.

Land reform should be directed towards farmers through programmes which wean them from their reliance on government

There are important gaps in agricultural servicing which need to be addressed if small farmers are to challenge the dominance of established commercial farmers:

- Small scale commodity brokers are needed to help small scale farmers access the best markets for their goods: in some areas it may be feasible to offer contracts to consortiums of small scale producers to supply fresh produce to large buyers like schools, hospitals, hostels and mines.
- There are almost no technical support structures for urban agriculture. As informal peri-urban settlement continues to encroach on prime agricultural land, considerable opportunities exist for shack residents to make the most of farming opportunities.
- Extension services have very little contact with food garden and subsistence farmers.
- Technical support must be broadened to include skills like marketing, business management, financing and input purchasing
- Natural resource management receives only token attention in most areas, and advice provided is often grossly inappropriate to the circumstances of impoverished subsistence farmers. With rare exceptions – like the Mpumalanga based NGO, Eco-Link – there are no institutions actively addressing sustainable resource use for micro-farmers. Credible training should be integrated into farmer support programmes at all levels.
- Small scale farmers are likely to need multi-disciplinary support rather than agricultural training alone. Successful small farmer support programmes in other parts of the world stress the importance of skills in decision making and local institution building, negotiating skills and assertiveness training – particularly for women.

In view of the general neglect of small farmer development programmes, it is ironic to note that empowerment in some instances will require a reduction in institutional support. There has been a tendency among bantustan development corporations to foster passivity and dependence among their clients through the paternalism of their interventions.

De Wet notes that, in this context, land reform should be directed towards the empowerment of farmers by means of support programmes which gradually wean them from their reliance on government assistance in the fields of finance and infrastructural support (De Wet 1995). Some farmers will have to be allowed to fail.

Rural enterprise development

Effecting agrarian reform through the land reform programme is crucial to development, but it can hardly be expected to resolve the poverty and unemployment backlogs in rural areas now and in the future. Resource allocation also has to be directed to non-agricultural activities.

Entrepreneurial initiatives have to be harnessed to spread the benefits of the land reform programme beyond the immediate pool of direct participants.

Moreover, the positive impacts of the land reform programme on rural local economies will not be optimised unless local entrepreneurs are able to provide newly settled farmers with the goods and services they require. Rising demand for seeds, fertilisers, basic implements and fittings, building materials and a range of related household goods and services will provide rural entrepreneurs with a ready market for commodities.

Land reform promises to boost the prospects of informal and small scale rural traders and service providers in the immediate future through the injection of finance to beneficiaries of land pilot projects and, further down the line, with incomes generated by the beneficiaries.

Entrepreneurial initiatives could help spread the benefits of land reform beyond the pool of direct participants

Unless local service providers are able to meet local needs more effectively, the money will flow quickly back to the larger urban centres and perpetuate the 'cash desert' syndrome in which rural areas are caught.

At present, rural markets are badly neglected by retailers and service providers, mainly because of problems with access to capital to develop rural retail outlets, distance from the main supply sources, and perceptions that the returns will be slim. The result is that money brought into rural areas leaches out rapidly when people have to travel to urban areas to make their purchases.

An innovative response to the logistical problem of rural entrepreneurs is the concept of periodic markets

An essential component of rural economic revival will be to promote rural enterprise development to ensure that money brought into – or generated in – rural areas, remains there and continues to circulate in those areas to boost rural trading economies.

A host of small business support initiatives are in place around the country. Unfortunately nearly all are located in larger urban centres, and most premise their lending facilities on conventional securities. Important exceptions to this include the Rural Finance Facility, the Get Ahead Foundation, the Women's Development Bank and the Small Enterprise Foundation.

Nevertheless, small entrepreneurs in rural areas face extreme logistical difficulties which are beyond the support capabilities of most existing support ventures: lack of banking facilities, their clients' limited spending power, erratic telephone services, poor road access to their stores and to the nearest supply centre, inadequate support from traders' associations and difficult access to bulk discounting schemes etc.

One innovative response to this problem is the concept of periodic markets, currently being piloted in the Stutterheim and Sekhukhuneland areas. Its first premise is that most rural villages cannot yet support traders who supply the full range of goods and services that people seek in towns.

One remedy is to make services available in a settlement once or twice a month on designated market days, possibly scheduled to coincide with pension days. Traders would have access to a customer base with cash, and customers would have access to goods and services not normally available outside towns.

At the end of each market day, full-time traders would close down their stalls and move on to the next village for the next day's trading, while casual hawkers and service providers would wait for the return of the market a fortnight or month later.

The Market Society is not shy about its ambitions. It aims to provide farming inputs, farming produce, clothes, food, health services, library services, hairdressers, shoe repair stalls and so on, and argues that the rural local council should meet on market days to ensure maximum local participation.

Commercial banks

Commercial banks have no presence in remote rural areas, which they perceive as offering high risks and low returns. The absence of financial infrastructure seems to be creating a 'chicken and egg' situation for private sector investment.

The retail and manufacturing sector is waiting for investment from the banking sector in rural areas to provide the financial systems needed for them to conduct their business, while the banking sector is waiting for some measure of increased economic activity in rural areas before they invest in new infrastructure.

Solutions to this dilemma implemented elsewhere – notably in Zimbabwe – include the establishment of rural development banks by government, and tax incentives and subsidies to encourage commercial banks to establish outlets in rural areas (Forster 1995).

Rural community banking ventures are in their infancy, but offer attractive possibilities for partnerships between local communities, government and public financial institutions. At Kraaipan, in North West province, a rural bank is being piloted where local residents will hold 50% of shares.

Conclusion

> The Government should set up rural development banks and grant tax incentives and subsidies to encourage commercial banks into rural areas

The process of transforming and reorienting existing institutions is well underway, and the institutional structures and support services needed by people in rural settlements are receiving unprecedented official recognition.

But pressure and momentum for appropriate servicing will have to be sustained by rural people themselves, rather than depend on advocacy groups and NGOs based in the cities and bigger towns, whose resources are limited and whose organisational voice is currently muted.

If we are talking of institutional reorganisation, we need to ask who has the power to enforce it and who to resist it.

Quite apart from the organised opposition of high profile interest groups like conservative white farmers and the competing resource claims of vocal urban militants, it is important to remember the inert power of entrenched bureaucracies to stall, to obfuscate, to insist that their administrative procedures are observed at all times, and to centralise power and decision making.

By definition, bureaucracies perform best with routine tasks, rather than problem solving or meeting objectives measured in qualitative, not quantitative terms.

The LAPC's national survey reveals an acute shortage of people with the vision, skills and experience needed to initiate and lead local land reform initiatives on lean budgets.

The importance of popular organisation and democratic practice should not obscure the centrality of individuals with the abilities to focus and lead local initiatives. People with those skills are in fierce demand.

Often the neediest areas are the most neglected and under resourced. This raises one of the toughest questions facing policy makers: should scarce resources be invested where they have the best prospect of achieving objectives, or where need is greatest?

Effective institutional cross linkages will be crucial to the success of land reform. There is a rich mix of institutional resources for the land reform programme to draw on.

There are countless assertive local organisations who can identify local needs but cannot address them, government agencies with funds and authority but limited experience, NGOs with experience but limited funds and staffing, and commercial agencies with skills, staff and flexibility but no mandate. What is missing is coordination, and a clear vision of objectives.

One of the greatest challenges of the land reform programme will be to gauge the right mix of institutional support to meet local needs: enough support to provide new farmers and rural residents with the inputs and backup they require, but not so much that it stifles initiative through over zealous intervention.

The key to effective institutional support will be to ensure that participants in rural development initiatives control the process themselves as much as possible, and to support them in their efforts to make the best use of opportunities.

One of the greatest challenges of the land reform programme will be to gauge the right mix of institutional support to meet local needs

CHAPTER TWELVE

THE PROVINCES

Land reform policies need to have national coherence, but implementing them on the provincial and local levels will depend very much on the peculiarities of each area. This chapter focuses on the provinces to get a general feel for their unique characteristics and their differences. There will be a brief look at their physical attributes, people and economies, and the challenges they face.

Land reform on a local level will depend very much on the peculiarities of each area

Geography of the provinces

Detailed geographical information was reported in nine provincial overview reports commissioned for the land study. The information highlighted important differences between and across provinces.

The size of the provinces varies greatly, with the smallest province Gauteng (18 760 square kilometres) and the largest province, the Northern Cape (363 389 square kilometres), also displaying the highest and lowest population densities respectively. KwaZulu-Natal has the largest population and is the third smallest province (91 481 square kilometres) after Mpumalanga and Gauteng.

The physical and climatic make ups of the provinces are markedly different. This is also true within provinces, which display a variety of agro-ecological differences.

Physical landscape determines the possibilities for development. The nature of the landscape defines the likely implications or consequences of different land use activities. Strategic questions on land use must be considered on a regional scale to ensure that land use decisions are logical and sustainable.

The Western Cape is characterised by a variable winter rainfall, with high rainfall over much of the south west, moderate rainfall in the southern Cape (all year) and low rainfall over much of the west coast and interior Karoo. There are also three distinct agro-ecological zones: mountain and lowland *fynbos* in the south west, succulent and arid Karoo in the north west, and the interior and indigenous forest of the southern Cape.

Rainfall in the Eastern Cape varies from between 400 millimetres to 1 000 millimetres a year. The topography consists mainly of sloping land, with mountains making up 31,3% of the total area and plateaus, plains and dissected river valley systems making up the rest. Even on the plains, extensive areas of level land are rare, limiting the availability of land suitable for cultivation to scattered pockets.

The whole of the Northern Cape is semi-arid to arid, with temperature extremes and little rainfall. There is not an extensive river drainage system and, besides the Orange and Vaal Rivers, most other rivers are non-perennial. As a result, the Northern Cape can be said to display very low levels of agricultural potential: of around 29 million hectares of farm land, fewer than 500 000 are classified as arable land.

The Free State is the most central province, bordering six provinces and Lesotho. Although it does not have its own metropole, it is centrally situated in relation to all of South Africa's metropolitan areas. The climate changes from east to west and even from year to year. Rainfall varies from between 600 millimetres and 700 millimetres in the eastern Free State to 250 millimetres in the south west. The central and western areas are characterised by low rainfall, high daytime temperatures and high evaporation rates, leading to a very harsh and arid climate.

Strategic questions on land use must be considered on a regional scale to ensure that land use decisions are logical and sustainable

In contrast, Mpumalanga experiences fairly high mean rainfall levels ranging from 600 millimetres to 1 100 millimetres a year. However, locally – particularly on the leeward side of certain mountain escarpments – precipitation can be below 500 millimetres a year. Mpumalanga contains a comparatively high level of medium to high potential soils which are conducive to agriculture.

The southern areas of KwaZulu-Natal enjoy high rainfall, low evapo-transpiration, good soils and under developed irrigation potential. The upland areas also have a favourable geo-physical climate for agriculture relative to other parts of South Africa, with higher rainfall, less rainfall variation and adequate water sources combined with a reasonable distribution of high potential soils.

In contrast, in the northern parts of the province a combination of low rainfall and high evapo-transpiration, together with limited availability of high potential soils and irrigation potential, suggests that prospects for substantial agricultural development are poor.

Access to water resources is often a source of conflict in most of South Africa's provinces

Lack of water availability is one of the most important constraints on development in Northern Province. Water supply infrastructure lags behind the level of demand from a rapidly growing population. Only 7% of Northern Province receives more than 700 millimetres of rainfall a year, while 45% receives less than 500 millimetres.

The North West, too, is prone to frequent droughts. In fact, the entire province is defined as having an acute desertification risk. The vegetation in the east is shrubby, otherwise grassland dominates. Rainfall is scant and erratic, ranging from less than 200 millimetres to 750 millimetres a year, exposing rain dependent farming to great risk. Despite this, the North West produces 35% of South Africa's maize output.

Gauteng has a mean annual rainfall of 668 millimetres, and suffers frequent water shortages. Since the province is quite small and highly urbanised – 96% of its people live in urban areas – there is comparatively little land available for farming. Grazing and rainfed crop production are the most important agricultural land uses in the province.

Access to water resources is often a source of conflict in most of South Africa's provinces. In Mpumalanga, for example, the conflict is fundamentally between upstream users who tend to be white commercial farmers located in the highveld, and downstream users who are black farmers living in the former homelands of KaNgwane, Lebowa and Gazankulu in the lowveld.

The Water Act allowed for the formation of irrigation boards which were to manage the distribution of water independently of government. In the Hazyview area of Mpumalanga, white farmers systematically organised themselves into irrigation boards and thus controlled the distribution of water from the Sabie river catchment.

Water for agricultural use is also a contentious issue in the Coloured Rural Areas of the Western Cape, where communities have had previous water rights curtailed or where access has been slowly eroded through increased usage by commercial farmers. Water availability and its distribution are common problems, and are exacerbated by the neglect of infrastructure such as canals, dams and irrigation facilities. Genadendal and Suurbraak are examples of Coloured Rural Areas with high rainfall and access to perennial streams, where poor infrastructure inhibits agricultural input.

Farming under irrigation takes place along the Orange and Vaal river systems in the Northern Cape, which are the two perennial rivers flowing through the region. The Vaalharts irrigation scheme is the largest contiguous irrigation area in South Africa. It delivers an agricultural lifeline to an otherwise semi-arid and arid region.

Water supply to rural settlements in the Eastern Cape is totally inadequate. For example, only half of rural residents in former Ciskei have access to adequate bulk supply by means of boreholes. Fifty percent of rural households, therefore, depend on open surface water such as rivers and dams to satisfy water needs which are often shared by livestock.

Land use

Land use potential and actual land use depend on a range of factors which go beyond geo-physical constraints. Land which has the potential for agricultural production is frequently under utilised, while irrigation allows for cultivation in areas with insufficient rainfall. Land use is also affected by tenure rights, access and land allocation.

South Africa is not well endowed with high potential crop raising land. Despite this, the country has a large agricultural sector, and a wide variety of produce. The Western Cape, KwaZulu-Natal and Mpumalanga contain substantial proportions of the country's arable land.

> South Africa is not well endowed with high potential crop raising land

The Western Cape is a major producer of fruit and wine, with all crops grown under irrigation. Other land uses include wheat – where rainfall is less than 400 millimetres – sheep and goats in arid zones and, where pastures under irrigation can be established, dairy farming and commercial and indigenous forests.

KwaZulu-Natal is relatively well endowed with natural resources and has a medium to high agricultural potential: more than three quarters of the total area of the province is potential farmland. Some 17% of agricultural land is potentially arable, 6,5% is best suited to forestry, and the remainder is classified as natural pasture.

In Mpumalanga, two thirds of the total area is potential farmland, of which a fifth is arable. A large amount of land has also been devoted to nature conservation and forestry, mainly towards the north eastern parts of the region.

Agriculture, mining, nature conservation, settlement and industry are the most important uses of land

Despite South Africa's generally low agricultural potential, every province reports that agriculture is a significant land use. In the Northern Cape, commercial agricultural production is the dominant land use activity, principally for extensive livestock production. Even in urbanised Gauteng, 40% of the surface area is devoted to commercial agriculture.

Other important land uses are mining, especially in Gauteng, North West, Northern Cape and the Free State, nature conservation in the Northern Cape and Mpumalanga, and settlement and industry in Gauteng and KwaZulu-Natal.

Tenure

Tenure rights and tenure forms across the country are differentiated according to race, and the pattern of land ownership and variety of available tenure differs from province to province.

In the former KwaZulu area of KwaZulu-Natal, 85,5% of land falls under the traditional communal tenure system, with small patches of quitrent and freehold. In the former Natal areas, freehold tenure is dominant.

In the Western Cape, private freehold tenure is the norm in the commercial farming sector. Small pockets of land in Coloured Rural Areas are communally owned but held in trust by the state, churches or private trusts. A similar pattern occurs in the Northern Cape, except that Coloured Rural Areas are fairly extensive, particularly in Namaqualand.

In the Eastern Cape, too, there are major differences between the old Cape province and former homelands. Most land in the former Cape is held under freehold title and portions of land are held by the state. In these areas it is generally easy to determine the status of a particular parcel of land, with the exception of 'black spots', which are held under quitrent title.

Generally in all provinces, formerly 'white' areas are dominated by registered freehold, leasehold and other forms of co-ownership, while formerly 'black' areas feature a variety of tenure systems including communal tenure, trust tenure, quitrent and freehold.

Land availability

The state is clearly the most important land owner with whom land restitution and redistribution claims can be negotiated.

However, state land has been alienated in a number of ways, most notably through privatisation. Privatised land includes tracts now managed by state corporations such as Transnet, Telkom and Eskom, and is best described as public land. In this context, municipal commonages and land assigned by the state to land uses such as dams, military bases and nature reserves, must also be assessed as public land.

In the Eastern Cape, several categories of public land have been identified but in many districts there is not a great deal of it, with the possible exception of land acquired for consolidating the former Ciskei and Transkei bantustans.

In the Free State an estimated 30 000 hectares of land is not fully utilised, of which 14 000 hectares is state land which has not already been allocated and 15 000 hectares is held by the Land Bank. However, the land is generally not high potential or suitable for small scale crop farming.

Tenure rights across the country differ according to race, the pattern of land ownership and variety of available tenure

The availability of private land depends on the price that can be paid for it. Evidence suggests that there is no shortage of land available on the market, with up to 4% of farm land transferred each year. In the Eastern Cape, an average of 500 farms change hands each year. In the Border region and districts adjacent for the former Transkei, researchers reported that many white farmers were selling up for fear that their farms would become 'unfarmable' and 'unsaleable'. In the Free State, an average of 4% of land is transferred annually and market values of land have declined in real terms in the last decade.

In KwaZulu-Natal, 2,5% of farmland was transferred in 1992 and 1993. Just over half of the sales were farms of less than 100 hectares and involved 14% of the total land in this unit size group. This suggests that the market for smaller farms is more buoyant than that for larger farms in the province. The average value per hectare of small farms was eight times higher than for larger farms.

In the Northern Cape, price information available indicates a general trend of low prices in western parts of the province – as low as R60 per hectare for grazing land – to higher prices in the east and southern Karoo areas of up to R230 a hectare.

> The state is clearly the most important land owner with whom land restitution and redistribution claims can be negotiated

People of the provinces

People are where they are because of past policies and practices. Influx control and forced removal made the greatest impact on the movement and location of people. Levels of poverty can be directly attributed to where people are located and their ability to access employment and services. For this reason, it is important to get an idea of numbers of people, how fast populations are growing, their age distribution, where they live and how they make a living.

South Africa's population figure varies from one source to the next, but is generally accepted to be about 40 million spread over all the provinces.

KwaZulu-Natal has the largest population – 8,5 million people – while Gauteng has the highest population density: 6,8 million people at 365 people per square kilometre. The Northern Cape has the smallest population and the lowest density: 763 900 people at 2,1 people per square kilometres.

However, average figures obscure the distribution of people within a province. In the Free State, for example, 22% of people live in former homeland areas where population densities are estimated to be 239 people per square kilometre, with some areas such as Witsieshoek in Qwaqwa reaching 1 000 people per square kilometre by the end of the 1980s. In the Western Cape, on the other hand, two thirds of people are concentrated in and around the Cape Town metropole.

Urbanisation is a crucial factor. In KwaZulu-Natal, nearly two thirds of people are found in rural areas. Although urbanisation is taking place and the proportion of people living in the countryside is expected to decline, absolute numbers in rural areas are not expected to drop.

The term rural does not reflect the shading off of urban into rural areas found in many parts of the country. As detailed in earlier chapters, there is rapid urbanisation in many small towns and migration towards cities: it is often not clear where a rural area ends and a dense rural or urban settlement begins.

The Western Cape is characterised by a dominant metropole with more than 140 scattered urban settlements, and with three centres larger than 50 000 people. The rural parts of the province are largely made up of the commercial farming sector and small coloured rural areas scattered through the region.

In the Northern Province, most people live in about 1 500 scattered villages which have an average population of fewer than 4 000 people. The province has the lowest rate of functional urbanisation in the country.

All the provinces, except the Western Cape and Northern Cape, include former homeland areas. All except the Free State have experienced boundary changes. In several instances boundaries are still in dispute.

The movement of people in and out of provincial borders describe linkages between the provinces. Gauteng is noted for in-migration, receiving migrants from nearly every other province, and there are strong economic and cultural links between it and North West.

The former Transkei region of the Eastern Cape experiences high levels of out-migration, with two thirds of its labour force employed in the South African economy outside the region. A quarter of South Africa's mining labour force is from the Transkei.

The Free State and Mpumalanga also receive migrants, notably from neighbouring countries. The southern Cape region and the Western Cape metropole receive migrants from the Ciskei and southern Transkei regions of the Eastern Cape, while the Northern Cape has experienced a steady drop in population due to the decline in mining and the poor performance of the provincial economy.

> Levels of poverty can be directly attributed to where people are located and their ability to access employment and services

A number of provinces have observed strong trends in urbanisation and migration. The Free State, Eastern Cape, KwaZulu-Natal and North West all report increased urbanisation.

In the Eastern Cape and Free State, large increases in the size of small towns have been reported since the 1990s, explained, as mentioned, by the decline in agricultural employment because of drought and retrenchment in the mining sector.

In KwaZulu-Natal both greater permanent migration as well as short term – weekly or daily – migration have been observed. Proximity to transport routes determines the length of migration. Increased rural-urban commuting on a daily, weekly or longer basis has also been observed in the Western Cape, with commuting facilitated by a good road infrastructure throughout the province.

Many provinces have strong trends in urbanisation and migration

All provinces except the Northern Cape experience positive population growth rates, which range from 1,7% in the Free State and Western Cape to 2,8% in North West. The average national growth rate is reported to be 2,2%.

Also, in all provinces the age pyramid shows a high proportion of people in the young and middle age groups. In rural KwaZulu-Natal more than 52% of people are younger than 15 years, while in Mpumalanga and Northern Province, 38% and 49% respectively are in this age group.

An analysis of income levels and distribution shows huge discrepancies, particularly between urban and rural people, men and women, and white and black people.

In Northern Province, 40% of households have no permanent source of income and another 40% earn below R800 per household a year, while real unemployment is estimated at 48%. A mean household income of R788,31 per month was reported for all rural areas of former KwaZulu in 1992.

The Development Bank of Southern Africa (1993) found that in 1991, 45,8% of the non-urban population in Mpumalanga received no income at all. In former KaNgwane the figure was 69,2% and 77,3% of women received no income.

In the Northern Cape, an analysis of unemployment figures shows clear racial and gender disparities. In urban areas, about 50% of African people are unemployed. However, African men experience 39,4% unemployment while 49% of African women are jobless. The corresponding figures for coloureds and whites are 25,5% and 7,2%, and 54,2% and 11% respectively.

The provincial economies

An understanding of the importance and structure of the agricultural economy in each province is essential in assessing the potential for agriculture to contribute to the development of the rural economy. Agriculture employs a substantial proportion of rural people throughout South Africa, although declining, low or negative growth in the sector has contributed to unemployment, poverty and urbanisation.

Agriculture is one of the main pillars of the Mpumalanga economy, along with manufacturing, mining and electricity. In 1991 it was the fourth largest contributor to the province's Gross Geographic Product (GGP), contributing 10% of total value of GGP.

The agricultural sector is highly diversified and the region is comparatively advantaged in the production of a large number of agricultural products. The largest contributor is livestock, followed by field crops, with horticulture and forestry also making significant contributions.

The Northern Cape economy is dominated by mining and agriculture. Agriculture contributed 11% to GGP and is the single biggest employer of labour. Manufacturing activity is relatively undeveloped in the province, and with the downscaling of mining activity associated with depletion of mineral reserves, the economy is experiencing declining growth rates.

Economic activity in the Northern Province is unevenly distributed geographically. Rural areas are characterised by a large and relatively unskilled population. Many thousands of people were dumped in rural areas of Northern Province under apartheid's forced removals, without infrastructure or hope of employment.

The informal sector contributed 30% of GGP in 1991, while the second largest contribution – 25% – derived from community and social services. Neither activity generates significant economic growth, as the former is essentially survivalist and the latter involves public sector salaries and government consumption expenditure.

> An understanding of provincial agricultural economy is essential to assess the potential of agriculture to the development of the rural economy

Agriculture contributes about 18% of GGP. However, since the mid-1980s, agriculture has declined largely as a result of ongoing drought and it currently employs 85 000 people, down from about 125 000 a decade ago.

The most important economic sectors in the Eastern Cape are manufacturing, agriculture, finance and transport. Agriculture offers 18,5% of formal employment in the region. Livestock production contributes three quarters of agricultural income, followed by horticulture. Communal farming is practised in 74% of former Ciskei and 84% of former Transkei. Despite its relatively small contribution to average rural household income, agricultural resource utilisation represents a valuable on-site economic activity. About 20% of households raise nearly all the cattle, half of all the sheep and a third of the summer crop.

Each of South Africa's nine provinces face unique challenges within which land reform needs to operate

Commercial agriculture currently contributes 6% of GGP in KwaZulu-Natal and 19% of national agricultural Gross Domestic Product (GDP). But it provides only 11% of formal employment.

Subsistence cultivators are estimated to contribute just 2% of reported GGP output from agriculture. If one takes downstream activities in the manufacturing sector into account, approximately 15% of the value of KwaZulu-Natal's output is produced from agriculturally related activities. The major agricultural activities are in the areas of animal and animal products, followed by horticulture, forestry and other products. Sugar cane is the dominant field crop, accounting for 95% of production and 79% of gross income from field crops.

Commercial agriculture is one of the key economic sectors of the Western Cape, contributing 10% of the province's GGP. If the Cape metropole is excluded, agriculture contributes 25% of GGP for rural areas, and in some districts the figure is over 50%.

The Western Cape also produces 20% of the gross value of agriculture in South Africa, most of which is generated by export crops like deciduous fruit, table grapes and wine. From 1985 to 1990 the sector experienced a 5,1% annual growth rate. It provides 38% of formal employment opportunities in rural areas of the province.

The most important economic sectors in the Free State are mining, commerce, manufacturing and agriculture. Agriculture contributes around 14% of GGP and 14% of formal employment. The economy experienced a negative growth rate of 0,18% between 1980 and 1988, and a decrease of 3,19% a year in agricultural employment between 1980 and 1991.

In the 1980s the total area under field crops in the Free State declined as a result of economic and climatic factors, while livestock and horticultural products became relatively more important. As a result of deregulation, the area under maize is expected to decline further, and diversification towards other field crops will take place.

Agriculture generates less that 1% of Gauteng's GDP, employing 70 000 people. Animal production contributes 77% of the province's agricultural income, and processing facilities are well established. Certain sectors such as animal production linked to feedlots and fruit production have expansion possibilities in Gauteng.

Despite its acute desertification risk, North West is a large maize producer and mixed farming occurs throughout the province, although stock farming predominates in districts of former Bophuthatswana and a large percentage of districts in the rest of the province are used for crop production. The North West economy is dominated by mining, which contributed 43,6% of GGP in 1991. Agriculture contributed 7,6% of GGP.

Provincial challenges

Each of South Africa's nine provinces face unique challenges within which land reform needs to operate. Land reform represents an opportunity to stimulate developments on a wide front.

Most provinces have to deal with the incorporation of former homelands and integration of huge numbers of civil servants into provincial administrations. In Mpumalanga, for example, there are five agricultural parastatals being merged to form the Agricultural Development Corporation. In Northern Province, some 700 field officers employed by three different former homeland parastatals provide extension services.

Low or declining economies and the impact of long term drought have taken their toll. The Free State has suffered declining agricultural and mining sectors, leading to problems of high unemployment, rapid urbanisation and poverty. The impact of drought is even greater in Northern Province, which has also had to contend with decades of under development. In the Northern Cape, declining mining activities place huge pressures on agriculture to provide employment and livelihoods to declining rural populations, while urban unemployment is increasing.

> All the provinces display large differences between urban and rural areas

All the provinces display large differences between urban and rural areas in terms of unemployment, income generating opportunities and living conditions, rapid urbanisation within provinces and in- and out-migration between provinces and beyond the country's borders.

PART THREE
POLICY

CHAPTER THIRTEEN

THE CONSTITUTIONAL INTERLOCUTOR

Between the many sided demand for land, the contest of interests and the possibilities of government action, there is the Constitution.

> A Bill Of Rights talks to society and informs it not only of what kind of society it is, but also of the one it ought to be

The Constitution is the supreme law of the land. It binds everybody and all institutions to a set of rules which establish rights and shape conduct within the physical boundaries of South Africa. As such, in a very general way it is both the expression of 'the will of the people' and the key arbiter over conflicting interests and rights.

Within the Constitution, the Bill of Rights is particularly important because, as Davis *et al* point out (1994), it is the link 'between the political morality and aspirations of a society and positive law', giving a particular set of political convictions legal sanction and constraining competing moralities which are inconsistent with them. It does this in the name of the people, rather than of the government of the day.

> *"Furthermore, unlike ordinary legislation, a Bill of Rights talks to society and informs it, not only of what kind of society it is but also of the one it ought to be. It contains not only constraints but also aspirations."* (Davis 1994)

The constitutional process began with the unbanning of political opposition in South Africa on February 2, 1990, and the Groote Schuur Minute of May 4 that year. Political organisations began negotiating the framework for a new and democratic South Africa in two forums – the Convention for a Democratic South Africa (Codesa) I and II – between December 1991 and May 1992, when Codesa collapsed.

The Multi-Party Negotiation Process got underway at Kempton Park in March 1993, and saw the transitional process through to agreement on an Interim Constitution on November 17 that year and South Africa's first democratic elections on April 27, 1994.

The Interim Constitution, the Working Draft of the new Constitution and the final Constitution, scheduled for adoption in May 1996, thus represent the outcomes of a very short and intense open political engagement which, for the first time, placed constitutionalism on the South African agenda and brought the country into the modern world.

The emphasis in the documents on equality and non-discrimination, fundamental rights, separation of powers, an independent judiciary and national unity as well as historical redress and future reconstruction for the creation of a sovereign democratic state, have swept away the pre-1990 constitutional legacy of:

> *"...parliamentary sovereignty, a dominant executive, indiscernible separation of powers, underdeveloped political accountability, no Bill of Rights and finally, a racist base".* (Van Wyk 1994)

At the same time, the constitution making process was part of ongoing political and social struggles deeply rooted in our past. It brought with it a heritage of unresolved or unsatisfactorily resolved issues which have influenced the shape and content of the new constitution as well as determined the ground for future constitutional and political contestation.

> The Department of Land Affairs emphasises problems arising from the allocation of powers and responsibilities between national and provincial government

Constitutionally, there are a cluster of issues which have a direct bearing on the scope and capacity of government to develop and implement policy on land, precisely because they reflect unresolved countervailing interests found in society at large.

The Department of Land Affairs, drawing on the difficulties it has had to face around implementation, places most emphasis on problems arising from the constitutional allocation of powers and responsibilities between national and provincial government (Green Paper, February 1996).

The Department's concern is driven by the practical problems of delivery and the present constitutionally determined prerequisite of high levels of cooperation and coordination between national and provincial governments, and between government line functions.

> **"Allocation of Land Related Responsibilities"**
> **Green Paper February 1995**
>
> "Land matters and legislative powers regarding land matters are a competence of National Government in terms of the Interim Constitution. Political accountability for land affairs lies with the Minister of Land Affairs.
>
> "Provincial Governments have legislative powers regarding a range of land related Schedule Six functions and political accountability for the performance of these functions. Schedule Six functions include: agriculture, environment, soil conservation, housing, regional planning and urban and rural development.
>
> "Local governments also have legislative powers regarding certain land and land related functions which they have to perform.
>
> "Tribal authorities, observing systems of traditional law, likewise perform certain land functions in terms of the powers and functions given to them by indigenous law, as well as by the administrations that operated in the former homeland areas.
>
> "The Minister of Land Affairs has been assigned numerous land related legislative measures for his administration. His executive department, the Department of Land Affairs, has been tasked with setting national land policy, embodying it in legislation, establishing land programmes, and implementing and funding them.
>
> "The Department also performs certain land administration functions emanating from land policies, legislative frameworks and land assets vesting in national government. A large percentage of these functions will eventually be assigned or delegated to other tiers of government."

Institutional coordination for effective implementation can be a site of social struggle, not merely a technical issue

To dismiss these complex issues as merely technical – and therefore as something that can be simply sorted out – is to miss the underlying tension in assumptions about policy making and execution in a politically and socially heterodox society.

Not only is institutional competition economically and politically intrinsic to the present organisation of government – both between and within different levels of government as well as line functions – but government is also the arena of larger conflicts between different social interests in the broader society. As such, the problem of institutional coordination for effective implementation is that it is a site of social struggle, not merely a technical issue.

From a perspective concerned with the Constitution as the basic law which establishes basic rights, the area of prime importance and a source of much controversy is the clause on property.

While many of the arguments have been persistent throughout negotiations, there appear to have been important shifts in direction and emphasis in the debates around property since the adoption of the Interim Constitution. There, property and land rights are dealt with in two sections.

The basic property clause is found in the chapter on fundamental rights. Section 28, Chapter Three establishes the right to acquire, hold and dispose of rights in property, prohibits unlawful deprivation of rights in property and provides for expropriation for public purposes. A second set of provisions regarding property are found in Sections 121 to 123. They give constitutional force to the provision of redress for the victims of acts of dispossession due to discriminatory laws and practices.

Unable to arrive at an acceptable agreement, the Working Draft of the New Constitution (November 22 1995) was released with three options – as well as a tentative separation of land rights from property rights by adding land to housing in Section 25 with a proposed Clause 3 that:

> *"...everyone has the right to have equitable access to land. The state must take reasonable and progressive legislative and other measures to facilitate this access."*

> From a perspective concerned with the Constitution as the basic law which establishes basic rights, the area of prime importance is the clause on property

While all options presented for debate accept the right to property, to the protection of land ownership and to the need for land reform (Report by Technical Advisers), they present these rights and their protection somewhat differently.

The first proposition is the 'no property clause' option. Up until the final rounds of debate in the Constitutional Assembly, all parties assumed that political realism dictated the need for a property clause in the Constitution – and that what was at issue was the way it should be formulated (Van der Walt 1994).

However, difficulties in arriving at an agreed formulation which would not simply protect vested interests but would also be open and flexible enough to allow for social and economic restructuring, gave weight to an earlier proposal that there be no property clause in the final Constitution.

Working Draft of the New Constitution (November 22 1995)

Property: Chapter Two, Section 24 – Options for Debate

Option One

No property clause

Option Two

(1) No one may be deprived of property except in accordance with a law of general application.

(2) Property may be expropriated only in terms of a law of general application

(a) for public purpose or in the public interest; and

(b) may be subject to the payment of compensation, within a period and in a manner as agreed by a court.

(3) When any court decides either the amount of compensation, or the period within or the manner by which payment must be made, the court must determine an equitable balance between the public interest and the interests of those affected, having regard to all relevant factors, including

(a) the current use of the property;

(b) the history and value of its acquisition;

(c) its market value; and

(d) the ability of the state to pay.

(4) This section does not apply to or invalidate measures aimed at bringing about land reform.

(5) Every person and community dispossessed of land after 19 June 1913 as a result of discriminatory laws or practices has the right to restitution of that land, or equitable redress, subject to and in accordance with national legislation.

(6) Every person and community whose tenure is legally insecure as a result of discriminatory laws or practices has the right to obtain legally enforceable security of tenure or, where appropriate, alternative redress, subject to and in accordance with national legislation.

The Draft Constitution proposes that those dispossessed of land after 1913 as a result of discriminatory practices have the right to restitution

Option 3

(1) Property, including the right to acquire, hold and dispose of property, is guaranteed.

(2) No one may be arbitrarily deprived of property.

(3) Property may be expropriated only in accordance with a law of general application

(a) for public purposes or in the public interest which includes land reform; and

(b) subject to the payment of just and equitable compensation, the amount, timing and manner of payment of which have been either agreed or decided by a court.

(4) When a court decides the amount, the timing and manner of payment of compensation it must equitably balance the public interest and the interests of those affected, considering all relevant factors including

(a) the current use of the property

(b) the history of its acquisition;

(c) its market value; and

(d) the beneficial improvements after its acquisition.

(5) Every person and community dispossessed of land after 19 June 1913 as a result of discriminatory law or practice has the right to claim restitution of the land or equitable redress subject to and in accordance with this section and a law of general application.

(6) In this section discriminatory law or practice means any law or practice that would have been inconsistent with Section 8 had that section been in force at the time the law or practice dispossessed the person or community.

Property is conceptually ambiguous and socially controversial, especially at a time of social and political change

Property is conceptually ambiguous and socially controversial, especially at a time of social and political change during which government commitment to social and economic restructuring needs to be legally reinforced.

The overriding effects of a property clause are likely to be negative, with arguments against its inclusion hinging around its reactionary effect – both because it tends to protect and institutionalise the status quo (Van der Walt 1994) and because, in so doing, it tends to obstruct and even actively block government reforms designed to redress historical injustice and social and economic imbalances (Report by Technical Advisers).

The experience of modern constitutions elsewhere has shown that a property clause can be well secured through ordinary land and property rights

Moreover, as the experience of modern constitutionalism elsewhere has shown, positive intentions behind inclusion of a property clause in a constitution can be well secured through ordinary land and property rights legislation, especially given a constitutional context where equality and due process clauses would make it unconstitutional to deal arbitrarily with property.

The second and third options both assume that there is a need for a property clause but they differ in important ways. The third option is essentially traditional, both in its insistence on a guarantee clause and in its formulation of an expropriation clause. Its underlying assumption harks back to what has been described as an outdated and unsuitable:

> *"...perception of property as an exclusive and unlimited private right which should not be interfered with".* (Van der Walt 1994)

Option three incorporated the argument about the need to give constitutional protection to the land reform process, but only with regard to restitution, and then in the narrow terms set out in the proposed section on property.

By contrast, the second option seeks to create a framework which incorporates and tries to balance individual and social interests. It drops a positive guarantee clause, recognising that such a clause is redundant where there is a negative expropriation clause which, together with other sections of the present and proposed constitutions, serve to guarantee individual rights (Van der Walt 1994).

The expropriation clause is put in a wider context, tempering market oriented strictures with broader, more socially relevant considerations. The second option also goes further with regard to land reform, covering both restitution and tenure security rights, although not extending to redistribution.

The proposal to include the right to land with the right to housing in Section 25 should be read together with the three options, and is contingent on the outcome of the property clause. By excising land from the property clause it aims to ensure land rights as a basic right, not conditional on any formulation under Section 24.

These options express – at the constitutional level – the social struggles over land rights and reform being waged in society at large. Considerable advance has been made in establishing the weight of social interest as legitimate and integral to a property rights system built on principles of justice and the protection of rights.

However, in this round of political negotiations it seems unlikely that it will be possible to achieve the best possible outcome for reform and development: that the final Constitution has no property clause.

Rather, almost in spite of the pressing need not to impede social redress, a clause on property seems most likely. In terms of its formulation, neither of the two remaining property clause options set out in Section 24 is likely to be accepted as they presently stand. Rather, the final outcome is more likely to be a compromise between the two – with land rights included. Effectively, it will still be a property clause which provides a guarantee of property rights while giving limited scope for social and economic restructuring.

Impeded reform

The consequences are likely to adversely affect government and community efforts to bring about change – especially on the land. It will be less than a vision of the kind of property regime South Africans would like to have, where the institution of private property is promoted as part of a wide range of divergent land rights.

Considerable advance has been made in establishing the weight of social interest as legitimate and integral to a property rights system

The final Constitution may well underscore ownership as the fundamental and most important right, and thereby reinforce existing vested interests. Instead of providing the moral authority for reform initiatives, it will then act to constrain them – conditioning access, limiting or even blocking reform initiatives, interfering with regulatory and other ordinary functions of government, opening up opportunities for costly and delaying litigation procedures etc (Report by Technical Advisers).

While some relief could come from the interpretation and emphases Constitutional Court judges give to the final Constitution, there is no guarantee that this will be the case. In this worse case scenario, not only will the highest law of the land impede government efforts to carry out reforms, but it will also fail to establish a legitimate system of property rights, fuelling conflict, violence and instability.

Traditional authorities

Another issue of importance for land rights and land reform is the entrenchment of traditional authorities and indigenous law as a distinct and separate system of law and governance within the final Constitution. A binding imperative of the Constitutional Principles adopted in the negotiating process, its inclusion reflects a 'common sense' political endorsement of a widely acknowledged institution in South African society, albeit of mixed acceptance and application.

What is understood as traditional authority and customary law today is far from the institution that characterised African societies prior to colonialism

Concerns with this approach are various, but perhaps most problematic is the fact that what is understood as traditional authority and customary law today is far from the historical institution that characterised African societies prior to colonialism. The recommendations of the Constitutional Assembly Commission on Provincial Government state that:

> *"...it seems clear...that the primary role of traditional leaders is in regard to the maintenance and application of indigenous law. Specifically, traditional leaders also have traditional powers in respect of the use and allocation of traditional land."* (Preliminary Recommendations on Traditional Authorities)

But to accept this is to invent modern arrangements infiltrated by colonial and apartheid land law and practice (Van Der Walt 1995) as if they were traditional customary law and practice.

On the one hand, research shows that chiefly authority was not always derived from control over land allocation. Rather, in some indigenous polities, as long as land was not a scarce resource, control was exercised in terms of rights over followers, tribute and cattle. On the other hand, allocation of land was one area of expansion that the colonial and then apartheid state permitted chiefs (Beinart in Banks and Southall 1995). The Constitution is therefore in danger of entrenching a very modern manifestation of an institution which, whether we look to the past or to the future, is problematic.

Without setting out exactly what the role or status of traditional authorities are, the final Constitution may well be interpreted as

Working Draft of the New Constitution (November 22 1995)

Traditional authorities: Chapter 11, Section 169 – recognition

(1) The institution, status and role of traditional authorities, according to indigenous law, are recognised.

(2) A traditional authority which observes a system of indigenous law and which was recognised in terms of legislation immediately before the Constitution took effect, may continue to function subject to any applicable legislation and customs.

(3) The courts must apply indigenous law when the law is applicable, subject to the Constitution and any relevant legislation.

Councils of traditional authorities: 170.

National or provincial legislation may provide for the establishment of councils of traditional authorities to deal with matters of common interest.

including their function in land allocation and control – what is and has long been a role underpinned by government (state) recognition. It may then serve to consolidate land allocation as their base of power and authority.

This will have negative implications for both democratised rural local government and land reform, and more generally for the success of 'mixed government' which aims to 'conserve traditional authority as a political resource without diminishing the authority of the state' (Dick-Sklar in Banks and Southall 1995).

> The final Constitution inclines towards historically vested interests, and does not address the needs of the poor in terms of land

If anything, the effective entrenchment of 'old order traditionalism' is likely to weigh against mixed government as a democratic form, precisely because it would require a major restructuring of rural government and the transformation of traditional authorities.

In short, while the final Constitution is likely to be a major advance on all of the previous constitutional frameworks that have guided South African society, its approach to key social issues and institutional arrangements inclines it towards historically vested interests. In this, it reflects more the present political balance in society and less a future vision which addresses the needs and aspirations of the poor majority – especially regarding land rights and land reform.

CHAPTER FOURTEEN

TENURE AND LAND REFORM

The Government has identified tenure reform as a major aspect of its land reform programme. In his speech to the National Conference on Land Policy in Johannesburg on August 31, 1995, Minister of Land Affairs Derek Hanekom set out five principles on which his approach to tenure reform was based. He described them thus:

> Freehold tenure has been the sole recognised tenure system by which people have been able to own land

- "Our starting point is that people must have security of tenure. That is what makes it possible for people to live in security, and to invest their energy and resources in land. We have to put an end to the system where people's land rights are dependent on the consent of someone with political power.
- "One of the legacies of the past is that many people hold land in a form which is not legally recognised, or is recognised in a very weak form. We need to ensure that these rights and interests in land are legally recognised and effectively protected.
- "We should not take an ideological position for or against individual freehold or communal forms of ownership. We should make a range of secure tenure options available, and enable people to make their own choices.
- "Tenure reform must give equal respect to the different rights and interests in land, of course in accordance with the content of those rights and interests. Where there are overlapping rights and interests in the same land, all must be respected.
- "Tenure reform must address a range of legal and other structures which prevent women from having independent access to land. Particularly, but not only in the rural areas, we often have the paradoxical and unacceptable situation that while the women are in practice the people on the land, they do not have any independent land rights, but have rights only through a male family member."

Since the introduction of Roman Dutch law and the institution of land title allied to survey, registration of title and a land market, freehold tenure has been the sole recognised tenure system by which people have been able to own land. Broadly speaking, land set aside as reserves for Africans was held in ownership by the state, in its various manifestations.

After the establishment of the South African Development Trust (Act 18 of 1936), most of the land set aside under the late and unlamented Land Acts (27 of 1913 and 18 of 1936) was vested in the Trust – and later, as the homelands were created, in the homeland governments.

Urban land was also not owned by African occupants but by the state, again in its various manifestations, or by white local authorities. Thus land was generally held under freehold tenure by the state, the Trust, a homeland government or a local authority.

Occupation of this land by Africans was either by way of lesser title or no title at all. For example, occupation on rural land held by the Trust or a homeland government was generally exercised by way of a Permission to Occupy (PTO) or, more often, under modified rules of traditional title deemed as being equivalent to a PTO. In the case of urban land, occupation was by way of Certificates of Occupation or lodgers' permits.

These systems depended on political patronage and protection and had little status in law, which was consistent with the control over land demanded by apartheid policy.

During the last decade Deeds of Grant and Rights of Leasehold – both less than ownership – were introduced and, following the former Government's 1991 White Paper on Land Reform, freehold title began to become available to Africans (Upgrading of Land Tenure Rights Act 112 of 1991 and the Less Formal Townships Establishment Act 113 of 1991).

> African people devised tenure forms – combining indigenous tenure with practical needs – which worked for people on the ground

As a means of coping with insecure or no title, African people devised forms of tenure which, while not legally recognised, worked for the people on the ground. These forms reflected a combination of indigenous tenure and practical needs, the precise mix depending on the locality of the land in question.

As the Minister pointed out, new tenure forms must reflect that reality and give legal content and protection to the diverse tenure arrangements that people understand and apply in their daily lives. We must seek African solutions to African needs.

Freehold and indigenous tenure

New tenure forms must recognise and protect the tenure arrangements that people apply in their daily lives

In considering types of tenure that might be adopted, it is necessary to compare freehold tenure with indigenous forms of tenure.

As was the case in most of colonial Africa, white settlers introduced an alien legal system to the colonies which, in 1910, became the Union of South Africa.

This was Roman Dutch law as applied in Holland during the 17th Century, and it forms the basis of our common law to this day (Holsten Edwards Natal and Bosman 1977).

The indigenous law (see end note) which governed the lives of the people already in occupation of the country was officially swept aside, but later selectively reintroduced in modified form as a means of administering and controlling indigenous people.

However, in the minds and practices of many indigenous people, including their descendants today, indigenous law continues to govern a major aspect of their lives. This also applies to land, its use and its occupation (Cross 1994). The duality in land tenure perception leads, inevitably, to confusion and conflict.

While the Restitution of Land Rights Act 1994 provides for restitution of land rights dispossessed as a result of apartheid laws and practices after June 1913, many claims are being articulated by those who make historic claims to land and rights to land arising from colonial settler dispossession. These claims appear not to recognise land titles issued in accordance with the common law, where titles were taken without the consent of the dispossessed.

The common law system of ownership is based on individual rights and obligations and, in so far as property in its wider sense is concerned, on private exclusive ownership. Put simply, if A is said to own a book, he or she has the right to control that book and the use made of it. All other people have the obligation to respect that right. This right of control, referred to in the common law as *dominium*, is central to the notion of the ownership.

The owner of land has the right to decide who may and who may not enter and remain on his or her land. In any court proceedings for the eviction of any person, all an owner need allege is that he or she is the owner of the land and that the defendant is on the land and does not have any right to be there.

The onus then shifts to the defendant to prove that she or he has a legal right – such as a lease, a lien or some other right – to occupy the land. Because of this notion of individuality, coupled with registration and state protection, freehold tenure promotes a land market and is a crucial factor in the accumulation of individual wealth. It also promotes landlessness and servitude.

Obviously, this right of ownership is restricted by the fact that the land lies in relation to other land, and the notion that land also has a social function. It is a common resource and has benefits and characteristics which entitle society to limit the absolute nature of the owner's ownership, the extent of such derogation being dependent on its locality.

Indigenous law, on the other hand, does not recognise individual ownership. In fact, ownership of the land in the common law sense of the word does not exist. Rather land is seen as a common socio-economic asset, administered by the lawful authority in the form of the chief, in consultation with the tribal council, for the benefit of the entire tribe or community.

Each member of the tribe or community has a right of access to land, to use it and to occupy it, governed by the laws and practices of the tribe or community. There is, however, no land market as land is not a commodity of exchange. Essy Letsoalo, in her book *Land Reform in South Africa*, says the following:

> *"Traditionally the North Sothos' land is not acquired through the market system as it is in...Western culture. Membership of the tribe is the qualification to obtain land."* (Letsoalo 1987)

Freehold tenure promotes a land market and individual wealth. It also promotes landlessness and servitude

Individuals have rights to occupy and use land according to the particular rules and practices of the tribe or community. But these rights are not exclusive and may be shared, in varying degrees, with others either within a particular extended family or within the tribe. Thus one person may have rights to cultivate land, but once the crop has been harvested, others have the right to graze cattle on the same piece of land. Gluckman describes it thus:

> *"...what is owned in fact is a claim to have the power to do certain things with the land or property, to possess immunities against the encroachment of others on one's rights in them, and to exercise certain privileges in respect of them. But in addition, other persons may have certain rights, claims, powers, privileges and immunities in respect of the same land or* property.

"Hence when we say that a particular group of kinsmen owns land, we are also saying that all the members of that group have claims to exercise certain rights over that land – maybe equally with one another, maybe varying with status. The incidence of rights over land varies with the technology of the tribe concerned, from those who live by hunting and collecting wild products to those who have elaborate systems of agriculture." (Gluckman 1967)

Indigenous law sees land as a common socio-economic asset, administered for the benefit of the entire tribe or community.

As was pointed out, Africans – particularly in the rural but also in the urban context, such as in informal settlements – have adapted the indigenous system to administer and manage the land they occupy.

They have done so partly through necessity under apartheid's restrictive land policies and partly because that is the system that is known and preferred. It is preferred because it recognises the social as well as the economic function of land and the interconnected relationships that exist between members of families and communities and which impact on land use and occupation.

These interconnections cannot be accommodated under freehold title (Coldham 1978). It therefore makes practical sense to seek a tenure form that recognises those realities.

The Communal Property Association Bill is one early and urgent attempt to provide a framework for communal ownership of land. However, it is predicated on the freehold system – now the only legal form of tenure – and as a result is cumbersome in approach and application.

A major consequence of the freehold system of tenure is its expense. It requires accurate survey and registration in a Deeds Registry with its attendant bureaucracy. It also supports an expensive – and unwarranted – professional class of estate agents, surveyors and conveyancers feeding off the system.

Land, as an essential social and economic commodity, must be readily and affordably available to all citizens and should not be the monopoly of any elite. While the abolition of freehold tenure in the legal system is not advocated, it should not be permitted to deny all people rights of access to land to satisfy their basic needs and to have reasonable access to natural resources.

As a starting point, therefore, the new land tenure regime must recognise the social as well as the economic value of land, and the right of all people to have access to it. Once that is done, a system can be constructed which will meet the basic needs of the people of South Africa.

The Minister of Land Affairs appointed a task team to investigate and make recommendations for tenure reform in South Africa. The team will take about two years to complete its work.

Coupled with the other legs of the land reform process – restitution and redistribution – and if successfully executed, tenure reform will introduce a more just and equitable land use policy to South Africa, in tune with the fact that it is an African country.

END NOTE

The formal term for indigenous law in South Africa is customary law, and it is useful to use that term when describing the distorted version of indigenous law recognised formally by the South African state. The term indigenous law, in this chapter, is used to refer to that law as understood and practised by people themselves.

CHAPTER FIFTEEN

THE CURRENT POLICY FRAMEWORK

Land reform is essentially a state initiative to modify, redirect or even change rights, usage and relations on the land – especially in rural areas.

Land reform is a response to pressures from below for historical redress and development

It has been a persistent feature of change in the 19th and 20th Centuries. Since World War II, land reforms have been undertaken as governments have come into office under the impetus of revolution, military defeat, the ending of colonial rule or a broadening of internal democracy. South Africa is no exception.

Following the first democratic elections in 1994, the ANC-led Government of National Unity identified land reform as a priority policy objective. It created the Ministry and Department of Land Affairs as a dedicated line function, institutionally responsible within government for developing and realising national land policy.

The purpose of this chapter is to review the framework that is being constructed to deal with the substantial and multiple needs for land among black rural and urban dwellers, and to analyse the role of the state in realising these reforms.

Pressures shaping policy

The framework that the Government is developing is influenced considerably by national and international imperatives. The need for land reform is internally driven. It is a response to pressures from below which come from two related sources.

The first is a widely held sentiment and expressed need for historical redress which is driven by the role that land dispossession has played in the oppression, disenfranchisement and impoverishment of black people, especially Africans. This is translated into policy as restitution.

The second is the pressure to initiate development which will address the widespread need for food, work, a place of settlement and improved livelihood strategies for the majority of rural people. In policy this is expressed in the redistribution and tenure upgrade components of land reform.

The shape and size of land reform is largely determined by pressures from above. Policy is significantly influenced by changing assumptions about what the state can or ought to do, and what its relationship with 'the market' and civil society should be.

Approaches to and debates around development – including land reform – in South Africa reflect the uncertainties about the role of the state which are part of a larger, global search for a strategy which redefines the balance between the state, the market and civil organisation: the major institutions of development (De Janvry *et al* 1993).

Impetus for change also stems from the need to develop good governance practices within the bureaucracy. The existing body of law and the way it is administered, needs to be rationalised and reorganised, given that:

> *"...the current system of land administration, inherited from apartheid, is chaotic. There is no single place in which all the myriad pieces of land legislation are all collected and accessible, and there is not even a comprehensive inventory of all the relevant legislation. In many instances, the authority which now has the power to make decisions is inappropriate, given the nature of the decision which has to be made."* (Draft Land Policy Principles 1995)

The shape and size of land reform is influenced by changing assumptions about the state and 'the market' and civil society

The sensitivity of the new state to these multiple, often divergent pressures is reflected in the approaches it has developed to land reform and the inherent tensions within it.

The policy framework

The most recent policy documentation from the Department of Land Affairs projects land policy reform as a complex and multi-faceted process which has at its core restitution, redistribution and tenure reform. In looking at the policy framework the focus will be on this core: what the Government's Green Paper of February 1996 termed 'the land reform programmes'. The way each of these strands of reform is being approached is historically and socially specific as well as being conditioned by the explicit guide rules which have been set out as principles underlying the land reform programmes.

The current system of land administration inherited from apartheid is chaotic

Principles of land policy

Green Paper on South African Land Policy February 1996

The following principles underlie the land policy of the Government:

Social justice

Widespread landlessness is one of the most lasting results of generations of dispossession and apartheid. Land is a basic human need. As a matter of simple justice government must take active steps to address this issue, deal with landlessness and remedy the unacceptably unequal distribution of land in South Africa.

Poverty focus

Priority is to be given to the poor who are in need of land to contribute to income and food security. This requires the identification of particularly marginalised groups in need of land, including women, evicted and existing labour tenants and landless farm workers. State assistance in land acquisition must be primarily given to communities and groups unable to enter the land market on their own. The financing arrangements for the programme must be structured to ensure access for people with little equity.

Needs based

Previous land policies operated from the basis of government designed plans and a supply driven approach. This resulted in inappropriate and unpopular programmes. To avoid this, it is necessary that the programme responds to expressed needs, and that mechanisms and structures are established to facilitate this.

Government as facilitator

Due to the marginalisation of the rural and urban poor and their weak organisation, the Government is concerned that the demands of the most needy cannot be articulated in an organised way. The Government is therefore committed to facilitate the expression of demand, and inform people about options. A clear and widespread dissemination of information about the land reform programme is vital.

Flexibility

Provincial and local variations across the country require flexible applications of policy within the framework of national norms and standards. Land reform policies need to be able to adapt in the light of experience and demand.

Participation, accessibility and democratic decision making

The participation of communities and individuals as partners with government and other agencies is necessary. Decisions must be taken democratically at local level. The extent to which this is achieved depends on organisation and capacity building, the establishment of sound and simple administrative processes to support land reform and the development of local government.

Gender equality

The land reform programme must bring about opportunities for equal access to and equal rights in land for women as well as men. The programme gives priority to facilitating the participation of women.

Economic viability and environmental sustainability

Planning of land reform projects developed at local level must ensure that these are economically viable and environmentally sustainable.

The restitution programme

The Restitution Act aims to restore land rights or to provide other forms of compensation to people dispossessed by racially discriminatory legislation and practice. Redressing historical land dispossession was enshrined in the Interim Constitution, and national Parliament enacted law – the Restitution of Land Rights Act 1994 – to meet this constitutionally derived obligation.

Redressing historical land dispossession was enshrined in the Interim Constitution

The Act creates a Commission on the Restitution of Land Rights, a Land Claims Court and general guidelines for dealing with claims. The restitution programme is expected to operate within a specific time frame: from the time of passing of the Act, there are three years to lodge claims, five years to finalise them and 10 years for the implementation of court orders.

The law creates specific boundaries which leaves:

> *"...limited scope for the Minister of Land Affairs and his Department to formulate further policy on restitution and restitution related issues". (Green Paper 1995)*

Principal national land reform laws

Green Paper on South African Land Policy February 1996

- The Restitution of Land Rights Act (22 of 1994), which provides for the restitution of rights in land to those dispossessed of land in terms of racially based policies of the past.

The Provision of Certain Land for Settlement Act (126 of 1993), which provides for the designation of land for settlement purposes and financial assistance for settlement support.

- The Development Facilitation Act (67 of 1995), which provides a mechanism for land development.
- The Upgrading of Land Tenure Rights Act (112 of 1993), to be amended, which provides for the upgrading of various forms of tenure into ownership. The Act provides for assistance in identifying the rightful holder, mediating disputes, and surveying and transferring land.
- The Land Administration Act (2 of 1995), which makes provision for the assignment and delegation of powers to the appropriate authorities.
- The Land Reform (Labour Tenants) Bill provides for the purchase of land by labour tenants and the provision of subsidies to this end.
- The Interim Protection of Informal Land Rights Bill is a mechanism to protect people with insecure tenure from losing their rights to and interest in land pending long term reform measures.
- The Communal Property Associations Bill will enable communities or groups to acquire, hold and manage property under a written constitution.

People have three years to lodge restitution claims, five years to finalise them, then over 10 years for the implementation of court orders

It is clear that the frame of restitution policy has been largely defined. This is so despite the fact that the documentation points to three outstanding concerns.

The first specifically relates to claimants excluded by the law, because they do not have a 'right in land' as defined by the Act, or were not dispossessed as a direct result of racially discriminatory laws but were affected by the processes these laws set in motion or, for instance, because they were dispossessed before 1913.

The response is an expressed commitment, through the terms of reference of the Commission and the broader policy framework, to address all cases of unfair dispossession 'even if the statutory mechanisms do not provide ready made solutions' (Restitution Act 1994).

Thus, for example, it is proposed to give labour tenants preferential status and financial assistance in land redistribution and land development programmes, and to accommodate pre-1913 land claiming communities at the discretion of the Minister.

It is also proposed to address those dispossessed by 'betterment policies' in the former reserves – which forcibly replanned people's settlement and land use patterns, through which many people lost land – through tenure security programmes, land administration reform and settlement support.

The second concern is about the scale and the nature of urban claims and the potential administrative, budgetary and development crises they could spark. To prevent the restitution programme from imploding the Government plans to deal with these claims on a group basis

And the third and related concern is the cost of restitution. The programme has major human resource, institutional and financial cost implications and these have not yet been fully calculated:

> *"The Restitution Commission is already facing an immense and time consuming task of registering, prioritising and investigating claims made thus far."* (Draft Land Policy Principles 1995)

There is a commitment to address all cases of unfair dispossession 'even if the statutory mechanisms do not provide ready made solutions'

The Department of Land Affairs hopes that these costs can be partially offset through inter-departmental cooperation at national, provincial and local government level.

Several observations can be made about the restitution programme. In the first instance, it has been built around a fairly swiftly established and broadly held consensus both on the need to address historical land rights and on the way this process should unfold.

Secondly, it is conceived of as a contained programme set within very specific social and time parameters. It is not regarded as a protracted process nor as a particularly socially disruptive process, although events may unfold differently.

Thirdly, because it is mainly rights driven, the restitution programme is not cluttered with complex concerns around production and economic sustainability, which are difficult to agree upon or realise. As the Department of Land Affairs has argued in response to concerns raised by the National Land Committee about exclusions generated by the existing law:

> *"Restitution should not be viewed as merely claims based and redistribution as needs based. Within an historical context both are claims and needs based and a coordinated cooperative approach is necessary."* (*Land Info* Vol 5, 1995)

Restitution is not regarded as a protracted process nor as a particularly socially disruptive process

The redistribution programme

Policy around redistribution, by contrast, is far less contained or settled. This is reflected most clearly in the Green Paper by the almost unnoticed but significant change in the order of presentation of the land reform programmes: for the first time in all available documentation, redistribution was prioritised over restitution in policy formulation. This said, however, much of the general direction that government wishes to pursue is fairly clear and established.

The Restitution of Land Rights Act 1994

Requirements set out by the Constitution and the Restitution Act.

- Claimants should apply to the Commission before May 1, 1998.
- The Commission will deal with all claims which qualify for investigation.
- To qualify, claimants have to have been dispossessed of a right in land or dispossessed under racially discriminatory laws or dispossessed without just and equitable compensation if expropriated under the Expropriation Act.
- Claimants have to have been dispossessed after June 19, 1913.
- The claimant should have a registered or unregistered right or interest which is not limited to ownership rights.

While documentation points to increasing emphasis being given to the urban component of land reform – which aims to ensure the provision of residential urban land close to jobs, transport and services – its primary focus is rural.

The stated purpose of the redistribution programme is to redistribute land:

> *"...to the poor, landless, farm workers, labour tenants, women and farmers for residential and productive purposes so as to increase their livelihoods".* (Draft Green Paper 1995)

The aim is to broaden and diversify participation in the rural economy while ensuring its growth. The main categories of people who are expected to benefit from the redistribution programme are set out in the box.

The plan is to execute the redistribution programme primarily through the market, adopting a 'willing seller willing buyer approach with expropriation as a last resort'. Direct state intervention will include:

> *"...the distribution of public lands and state spending on land development; direct state grants; state financed credit retailed through local finance institutions; and support to state and other institutions to administer land redistribution".* (Draft Land Policy Principles)

These measures will need to be responsive to social and economic needs, and to the creation of an enabling environment, which is expected to encourage previously disadvantaged individuals and groups to participate in the land market.

> The aim of land distribution is to broaden and diversify participation in the rural economy while ensuring its growth

Intervention will be conditional upon 'the benefits this will bring to the poor and the effects it will have on the macro economy'.

At the heart of the land reform programmes – especially redistribution and tenure upgrade – are a number of grants and services which, it is felt, will 'be capable of responding to a highly segmented land market'.

As to implementation, the state is seen as having a key indirect role: to facilitate and provide incentives for cooperation between itself and beneficiaries, the private sector and non-governmental organisations.

Beneficiaries of land redistribution and priority criteria

Green Paper on South African Land Policy February 1996

The following are the categories of people identified as potential beneficiaries of land redistribution, and the criteria for redistribution project prioritisation. The beneficiaries are listed in the Green Paper (1996) as:

- Landless people, including women, who wish to gain access to land and settlement opportunities in rural or urban areas.
- Farm workers and their families who wish to improve their settlement and tenure conditions.
- Labour tenants and their families who wish to acquire and improve the land which they hold or alternative land, in accordance with the proposed Land Reform (Labour Tenants) Bill.
- Residents who wish to secure and upgrade the conditions of tenure under which they live.
- Entrepreneurs who wish to acquire rural property for production purposes.
- Beneficiaries of the Land Restitution Programme in terms of the Restitution of Land Rights Act 1994 (22 of 1994) who require additional funds for meeting basic needs on restored land.
- Dispossession cases which fall outside the ambit of the Restitution of Land Rights Act 1994.

Redistribution projects will be ranked in priority order according to the following criteria:

- The most critical and desperate needs will command Government's most urgent attention. Priority will be given to the marginalised and to the needs of women in particular.
- In view of the limited institutional capacity to deliver and the need to reward initiative, priority should be given to projects where the institutional capacity exists to implement quickly and effectively.
- Viability and sustainability of projects must be ensured by attention to: the economic and social viability of intended land use; fiscal sustainability by the local authority; environmental sustainability; proximity and access to markets and employment; availability of water and bulk infrastructure.
- Government will ensure a wide geographical spread and a diversity of land redistribution projects through the country. Different types of beneficiaries, land uses and tenure arrangements will be supported in order to address the multiplicity of needs.

The plan is to execute redistribution primarily through the market, adopting a 'willing seller willing buyer approach with expropriation as a last resort'

There are two vehicles to carry through the redistribution programme. The first is the inherited mechanisms created by the previous government at the beginning of the 1990s through the Provision of Certain Land for Settlement Act 126 of 1993, which allows land to be set aside for rural settlement and provides financial support for communities to buy land for residential and productive purposes. Although various projects are being dealt with under this law and by this procedure, a review process is being undertaken to bring it in line with the new policy framework.

The second and main means of delivering the redistribution programme will be through the structures, mechanisms and experiences which are being developed in one district in each of the nine provinces under the Land Reform Pilot Programme.

The pilot process is seen as a first step to wider land reform which will spread fairly quickly – unconstrained by the pilot time frame – and which will build on and learn from the practical experiences gained through implementation.

The pilot programme is expected to show results within five years. Although the scale of redistribution has not yet been quantified, it is hoped that within 10 years there will be more far reaching positive effects of land redistribution.

The Green Paper talks with confidence about the ability of the market to redistribute land, suggesting only that 'responding even-handedly to each segment of the land market is likely to present a challenge'.

This signal of unease about the real tensions between different landed interests that are likely to arise in the programme, surfaces more strongly in the presentation of land tenure reform, and is arguably the explicit pressure shaping the direction of the debate around tenure – a discussion which will be picked up later.

> At the heart of the land reform programmes are a number of grants and services

The redistribution programme is principally strapped by economic constraints imposed by its foundation on the market. This is so despite the immediacy of institutional capacity problems which bedevil delivery – and which are not confined to limited state institutional capacity.

Buying into a market, which inherently inclines to upward rather than downward redistribution, is costly for the state and for the poor who need to access it.

Envisaged Grants and Services

Green Paper on South African Land Policy February 1996

The grants and three service facilities presently envisaged are:

Settlement/land acquisition grant

Set at a maximum of R15 000 per beneficiary household, to be used for land acquisition, enhancement of tenure rights, and investments in internal infrastructure, top structure and fencing, according to beneficiary plans.

Land acquisition grant

A land acquisition grant which can also be accessed by local authorities to establish agricultural lease schemes for residents of towns and villages is presently being investigated.

Settlement planning grant

To enlist the services of planners and other professionals, to assist beneficiaries in preparing project proposals and settlement plans.

District planning grant

To enlist the services of planners and other professionals for provincially supported planning of resource allocations for land reform and settlement on a district level.

Facilitation services

To ensure that eligible land reform beneficiaries have access to the necessary information and are able to seek access to appropriate services and assistance.

Training and capacity building

To encourage people to become actively involved in the land reform process and to equip both potential beneficiaries and service deliverers to participate more effectively.

Dispute resolution services

To prevent and, where necessary, to resolve land and land related conflict.

The state's main means of delivering redistribution will be through mechanisms developed under the Land Reform Pilot Programme

It is unlikely that the state will be able to find enough money to meet the need for land on the scale it is required, given the number of people wanting land, the use they want to make of it and the competition for resources within the state. As a relatively lowly prioritised project within the national budget – lying 22 in 38 allocations in 1995/1996 – the Department of Land Affairs points out that:

> *"...unless land reform can be shown to be alleviating rural poverty and contributing to economic growth, the necessary budgets will not be forthcoming". (Land Info* Vol 5, 1995*)*

Moreover, the ability of a large section of the rural poor to repay loan finance, should it become available, seems low, given their poverty and the scale and nature of their involvement in both agricultural production and formal sector employment.

But most importantly, the countervailing tendency to push people off the land – for example, through retrenchment, concentration of production in fewer hands, natural population increase etc – is likely to override state supported efforts to buy into the land market.

Land tenure reform

Land tenure reform is the third of the land reform programmes. Its express purpose is to clarify and strengthen the rights of individuals, families and groups to the land they occupy under diverse systems of tenure.

Like the restitution programme, tenure reform is essentially rights based, designed to extend registerable tenure rights to all landholders, to eliminate land holding systems based on permits and to ensure that holders of individual and communal rights in land – as land owners – have comparable status in law. Also, it is hoped that tenure security will contribute to:

> *"...personal security and social stability as well as higher levels of investment and more sustainable use of land and other natural resources".* (Green Paper)

The redistribution programme is principally strapped by economic constraints imposed by its foundation on the market

As a programme 'conceptualised fundamentally as a rights enquiry process', it is evidently supplementary to the restitution and redistribution aspects of land reform.

By emphasising the need for diverse forms of tenure 'including communal, group and individual ownership, on the basis of local preference', tenure reform is designed to create space in and control over the excesses of a landscape in which private property is the foundation of land rights. This means that communal or group tenure systems will be regularised and have full legal recognition.

> Communal or group tenure systems will be regularised and have full legal recognition

As much as tenure reform is needed, it will have difficulty succeeding on its own terms, especially with regard to group forms of ownership, given the institutional predominance of individualised and privatised tenure within the system.

At a generic level, the prospects of tenure reforms resolving the inherent tensions in the overall land reform project are even more elusive.

The concerns pose the challenge of what to do? The question is not simply whether these tensions can be resolved or not – since socially they will be decided, although not necessarily in the way the Department of Land Affairs (the state) would hope.

Rather, what needs to be strategised is the role that the state can play in proactively addressing tensions in order to generate outcomes which are consistent with its commitment to 'development'.

Locating land reform

Flowing from this review of the land reform programmes, there are several more general observations which need to be made about the overall policy approach before looking at the role the state might play in realising its goals.

The state seeks to reshape land relations in order to accommodate both welfare needs and the imperatives of growth to achieve 'development' in the broadest sense of the term. In this sense land reform is very much a product of the present structural and social conditions that exist.

Given the advanced state of agrarian transition in the South African countryside, where agriculture is organised overwhelmingly around wage labour based individual and corporate enterprises, two alternative courses present themselves.

One is to complete the process of detaching people from the land and entrench a small core of production around the existing commercial body corporate, with some limited black entry – the 'growth-efficiency model' as advocated by the dominant farming establishment.

The other is to actively curb, if not break, the push off the land through land (and agrarian) reform in order to encourage a broader production base which will both help people survive better and contribute to more generalised growth.

The state has opted for the second track, although the reasons why it has chosen to do so need to be looked at more closely. Historical redress is a politically explicit – but arguably small – part of the motivation. More significant by far are the pressures on the state to find economic answers to endemic and widespread poverty in order for it to retain credibility and legitimacy. As has been argued more generally about the modern state:

> *"...as political survival and internal peace are more often defined in economic terms, states have become responsible for economic transformation...The state's economic role goes beyond being a means to military ends. It is a source of legitimacy in itself..."* (Evans 1995)

In the absence of a social security net, hopes, if not efforts, are pinned on transformative economic initiatives, which only serve to aggravate the contradictions within the state, and society at large, over what can be termed 'welfarist' and 'growth' objectives.

These tensions are evident in the land policy framework. They are made explicit, for example, in the policy principles and the criteria set out to determine beneficiary selection and project prioritisation. And they are implicit in many of the assumptions which underlie the framework, some of which need to be examined more closely.

The result is that the prospects of overcoming the mountain of economic viability on an agricultural project basis, for the overwhelming majority of the poor who might be involved in the programme, are undeniably remote. This goal is made even more distant by the time constraints stipulated for the endeavour.

> The state is under pressure to find economic answers to widespread poverty in order for it to retain credibility and legitimacy

The tensions around making 'equity and efficiency' complementary in conditions where the needs of the poor and macro-economic considerations are more likely to be weighed against one another, forces another major assumption to the fore – this time external to the framework – namely, that it is achievable:

> *"...if a comprehensive strategy for the economy as a whole, which places land reform as a central force in the agro-industrial complex, is adopted."* (Green Paper 1995)

While this could be the case, the problem is that the 'comprehensive strategy for the economy as a whole' is not in place and the land reform policy framework is. In its absence, there is a real danger that all development needs will be channelled towards the land reform programme because it is there, causing it to implode under the strain of its limitations.

The absence of an economic strategy means there is nothing in place to help the land reform programme achieve its objectives

Alternatively, the absence of an economic strategy means that there is nothing in place to help the land reform programme achieve its objectives – either by relieving the pressure on the land because people have more viable alternatives, or by enabling people to use the land in a more effective way because they have access to resources external to the land reform programme and the agrarian sector more generally.

Another possibility is that a strategy may be developed by the state (not the Department of Land Affairs), which either goes against the specific directions land reform is taking, or significantly reduces the importance attributed to land reform, or is even against land reform *per se*. This is a real consideration given the limited potential of the agricultural sector to drive the national and international economy in a context where:

> *"...transformation is inescapably defined in global terms (and)...each nation's place in production for global markets has powerful implications for its politics and the welfare of its citizens."* (Evans 1995)

Role of the state

This brings the discussion back to the role of the state in development and the place it has assigned itself in land reform. The state sees its task as essentially facilitative of the market. It casts itself as playing a largely passive and subordinate role, although not a non-interventionist one, as the Department of Land Affairs's rebuttal of the National Land Committee (NLC) critique vigorously points out. To wit:

> *"The NLC proposal implies that the Government's land reform programme leaves redistribution open to the forces of the market alone. This is of course not true. The Government's land reform programme does involve state intervention through the provision of grants for land acquisition and the provision of basic needs and planning. Other supportive*

> *services such as facilitation, training and mediation are also part of the programme. We do not believe that the degree of state intervention suggested by the NLC is the best way to achieve land reform."* (*Land Info* Vol 5, 1995)

The question is not whether or to what extent the state should intervene in markets, but what kind of role it should play. The challenge, therefore, is whether 'facilitation' is the right place for the state to be. Are there not strategic options it could pursue around land and agrarian relations and in the broader economy which would make the economic aspects of land reform more viable?

Put another way, if facilitation brings the poor into the land market, as is hoped, what is going to keep them on the land in conditions where most will realistically only have access to small holdings on relatively marginal land? The present answer, limited as it is to the income they are able to generate off the land, is inadequate.

What is required is far more serious strategising around sustainability, giving due weight to the possibilities the state can help realise. In a similar vein, the state needs proactively to tackle conditions of employment in commercial agriculture – especially wages – given that it is the single largest source of formal employment in the countryside.

The inclusion of rural labour rights and the elaboration of settlement options which might be considered for farm workers in the Green Paper, introduces these issues for the first time into land policy thinking and is an important new step. However, practically they are still located in the programmes in narrowly defined terms (labour tenancy, housing) rather than in a more encompassing way which will touch the majority of farm workers who are not labour tenants and do not live on the farms where they work.

Far more serious strategising around sustainability is needed, giving weight to what the state can help realise

Recasting the institution of the state as a proactive agent of development brings to the fore another set of problems around institution and agency. With regard to institutional issues, the land reform policy framework makes a rather heroic assumption that somehow institutional weaknesses at state level can be compensated for by civil society.

In this, it is entirely in keeping with the current development vogue of institutional substitution, which especially sees civil organisation as an attractive means of filling the gaps in government programmes and expanding private sector activity.

However, some home grown experience – in the Land Reform Pilot Programme, for example – tends to portray a different picture, confirming observations of experiences elsewhere: that this assumption is a fallacy which tends to misjudge and over estimate the capacity of non-governmental and grass root organisations to deliver development.

Policy formulation and intervention is a struggle between different classes, groups and networks of individuals in all institutions at every level

Rather, they are often weak, with their weaknesses derived precisely from weaknesses inherent in the state. Institutional substitution is therefore not a practical answer. Instead, given that:

> "*...it is government policy framework which determines the effect civil organisations have on rural development. The issue therefore is not whether non-governmental organisations and grass roots organisations can substitute for government but rather how state policies can open the space for and take account of them without assuming inherent complementarity and compatibility.*" (Marcus 1994)

The state has been sharply criticised for its 'top down' formulation of policy and the implications this holds for implementation (Levin 1994). While it is misplaced to simply dismiss the Department of Land Affairs's commitment to 'participation, accessibility and democratic decision making' as well as 'partnership' as 'the language of participation as legitimation' (Levin 1994), concerns around participation and process raise the question of agency.

In formulating land reform policy, the state has to come to terms with the problems common to many states and development agencies, namely the relation between institution and agency.

From this perspective policy formulation and implementation are regarded as a largely linear process: decisions are made at the policy level, and they are translated into rules and procedures at the organisational level to produce the intended effects at the operational level (Cramb and Wills 1990).

The state's identification of institutional capacity as the 'most severe constraint presently bedevilling delivery' (*Land Info* Vol 5, 1995) – although a real constraint – may well be a misdiagnosis of the underlying problem. A critical review of policy failures and practical experiences suggests, rather, that:

> "*...implementation is often the most crucial aspect of the policy process, and its outcome is highly variable not nec-*

essarily because of limited institutional capacity or absence of a political will but rather because 'implementation is an interactive and ongoing process of decision making by policy elites and managers'." (Cramb and Wills 1990; Marcus 1994)

According agency its proper place, then, means that policy formulation and intervention has to be redefined for what it is: a struggle between different classes, groups and networks of individuals in all institutions at every level. It is ongoing, socially constructed and continuously negotiated. And the role of the state, as agency, places it in a far more critical and proactive position than the presumption of 'facilitation' allows.

In terms of its land reform objectives, the projection of the programmes as a 15 year engagement may well be a realistic reading of the time available to them before the crucial impetus within the state begins to wane. Then, as has happened elsewhere, land is likely to be absorbed into another line function. The need, therefore, is to focus the land reform policy, to redefine the role of the state as a proactive agency, and to strategise within and across institutions and at all levels to achieve the programme's stated goals.

Lastly, there is a need for the policy process to go back a step and re-examine a pervasive assumption which supposes a rural-urban dichotomy built around a division between agricultural production and urban settlement. This fallacy not only forces policy thinkers to discount their own observations about the evident rural need for and interest in a place of settlement, but it also misdirects their focus away from the key rural development issue.

From the perspective of development, the manifest 'deagrarianisation' of the South African countryside suggests that it is misdirected to concentrate on agriculture as the engine of future rural development. While broadening to an agricultural base will meet some production and welfare needs for some segments of the rural population, the needs of the majority are likely to remain unattended and as pressing as in the past. Rather, the state has to begin creatively developing other sectors of the economy to stimulate development in both urban and rural areas.

> The projection of the land reform programmes as a 15 year engagement may well be realistic

Thus, while widespread rural homelessness does have a negative impact on agricultural production, and is a planning issue as emphasised in the section on development planning in the Green Paper, what is notably absent in the documentation is the programmatic response needed to tackle such a major problem.

CHAPTER SIXTEEN

CONCLUSIONS

> The most universal and immediate land need is for a place to live, a home and a secure place of settlement

This first ever national study of the need for land in South Africa, undertaken almost concurrently with the process of political transition into a new democratic order, provides a revealing insight into current conditions – especially in the countryside.

Through the prism of land demand, the research simultaneously brings us up to date with the social changes that have been wrought on rural areas by political and economic processes over the past century, and establishes the starting point from which to initiate reform.

There is a large expressed demand for land. It encapsulates a range of felt needs, some of which are general while others are specific to particular strata of people and particular localities.

The most universal and immediate land need is for a place to live, a home and a secure place of settlement. Land for housing confirms an already recognised urban land need. But what is surprising – and what requires some explanation – is the importance of the need for residential land in rural areas.

This need signifies the extent to which political and economic changes in the countryside have lost poor people their homes, contributed to their impoverishment and forced changed patterns of settlement and livelihood. It also underscores the degree to which the majority of rural people are detached from commercial farming, the dominant agricultural land use system.

And it suggests that extensive rural homelessness – partly through lack of secure tenure – is not only reflected in an exodus to cities. A large number of people are settling in the service centres and small towns that dot the countryside.

Residential land need in rural areas, or among people who have recently moved off the land or who still have strong links with the countryside, is somewhat different from the land for housing need of urban industrial centres. Often it is strongly connected to production, especially agriculture. People are looking for a site for settlement which would include gardening and/or possibilities of running some stock on commonage.

Both features – the detachment from productive land and the desire to use residential land for production – resonate with the demand for land for agriculture.

Although currently this need is less significant in scale than the need for land for settlement, there is a substantial number of people in rural areas who want land to farm. Most people needing productive land are interested in the contribution it can make to household food needs. Many want garden plots which they can cultivate to provide food for home consumption.

Mostly it is women who want land for arable micro production. Men's agricultural interests gravitate towards livestock, although many women hold a few small stock. In terms of people interested in land to farm for the market, where surplus production is intermittent the gender mix is more balanced, becoming weighted decidedly in favour of men the larger the scale and the more substantial and sustained market production becomes.

The use of and interest in land for agriculture is best understood in terms of a production continuum, where there is some – at times considerable – movement between the different levels of production.

This mobility is determined by the coincidence of a range of changing factors, including climatic conditions, government policies, the size and composition of the household, and agricultural and non-agricultural employment opportunities.

When conditions combine favourably to create opportunities, there is a pull towards more surplus and sustained market production. Conversely, drought, land hunger and an adverse economic and policy environment push people into micro agricultural activity or out of the sector altogether.

> There is a substantial number of people in rural areas who want land to farm

Approaching agricultural activity as a continuum of levels and degrees of production along which there is two-way social movement, helps to locate a key regenerative source of new entrants into the commercial sector, and takes us away from a static notion of 'emergent farmers', which is somehow magically conjured into being. It also reveals the importance for many rural households of sustaining non-commercial production.

Mostly it is women who want land for arable micro production. Men's agricultural interests gravitate towards livestock

From a development perspective, what needs to be better understood in the South African countryside is the 'moment of critical mass' – the combination of conditions which push people into sustained commercial production at the one end of the continuum or, at the other end, out of agriculture altogether.

Land availability is not the only consideration. People's interest in land for agriculture is also conditioned by an astute understanding of other major constraints – particularly water, capital, labour and access to markets – which affect their ability to produce. Where conditions are adverse, people with limited resources adopt strategies to minimalise risk, which invariably reduces their use of and interest in agriculture.

These considerations underscore the dynamic and fluid nature of the need for and interest in agricultural land. It is conditional upon natural and social considerations internal to the dominant farming system, as well as upon alternatives presented by external, non-agricultural economic possibilities. Internal and external conditions are crucial to both drawing people off and keeping them on the land, attracting many people away from agriculture and allowing some to continue farming and expand their production.

The need for, interest in and use of land is socially stratified. Among the poor, the land hungry and the landless, there are differences which derive from their gendered historical, economic and physical location. While these differences are important in determining the nature of their land interest, they are often not fundamental.

The greatest social cleavage is between those who have land (and other resources) and those who do not. Present vested interests in land are also internally differentiated and variously derived. Largely they are centred in commercial agriculture, but they are also found in mining, tourism and nature conservation – and, importantly, in the traditional authorities system. Their relationship to the land needs and interests of people who are poor and often landless is far from homogeneous.

For a range of reasons which are inseparable from their size, space of activity and position in the market, the greatest innovation in agricultural land management needs comes from the corporate sector, particularly sugar and timber. While their motive is profit, they have chosen to pursue their interests in a way which offers considerable social and economic investment.

By contrast, the response of individual commercial farmers is more mixed. Many have begun to respond in an accommodating and innovative way, although most still react to land related social pressures as a threat to their enterprises which others must resolve.

Traditional authorities are more ambiguous. They are interested in mobilising around the land needs of the poor, since the poor are the source of *amakhosi* power in many parts of the countryside. But because this mobilisation is inseparable from enhancement of traditional authorities' personal land interests, they find themselves in conflict with the interests of the poor, resulting in often confusing, opportunistic social and political alliances and outcomes.

The research focused narrowly on institutions, concentrating on their capacity to facilitate land reform. At all levels, institutional capacity is uneven and often weak. Generally it tends to be weighted in favour of sections of society who have resources and who, for political and economic reasons, have been able to organise themselves to command institutional attention.

Not surprisingly, most poor, landless men and especially women in rural areas have very low levels of organisation and minimal institutional support. Where they are organised, more often than not it is through the hierarchically ordered, poorly resourced traditional authorities system where people's status, class and gender all influence their capacity to act and to be served.

This problem poses an enormous challenge to land reform. The significance of weak institutional capacity among the poor is not about whether there is capacity to see the reforms through, but about who determines the reforms and who sees them through. Institutional capacity, like land, is very unevenly distributed.

> If the people who most need land have low organisational capacity, it is doubtful whether their needs will be heard or met

If land reform is to be driven by demand – understood as an organised, expressed need – and the people who most need land have low organisational capacity, it is doubtful whether their needs will be heard or met. Countervailing organisational capacity is not likely to develop spontaneously nor, when it does, will it develop quickly. Aside from proactive state and state aided non-governmental organisation support, urgent consideration needs to be given to measures which can prevent only the rural elite benefiting from land reform.

The new Government's land reform programme is a deeply considered and committed initiative which is trying to address the huge, historically created backlog of needs and rights within a development imperative. It is a welcome development and one which will go a long way towards addressing the basic needs of the poor.

> The new Government's land reform programme will go a long way towards addressing the basic needs of the poor

Land reforms elsewhere have concentrated on changing the landed relations which underpin the structure of agricultural production. Clearly there is scope to broaden and change the presently narrow, racially cast production base that exists in the South African countryside.

However, even if these changes are optimally carried through, given political, demographic and economic constraints – as well as expressed interest in land – they are unlikely to draw the majority of rural dwellers into substantial agricultural production.

Realistically, a broadened and expanded agricultural sector is likely to incorporate some rural people into sustained commercial activity, while also providing opportunities to relieve the household food needs of many more through micro and occasional surplus agricultural opportunities. But the settlement and livelihood needs of most rural dwellers would remain unresolved, with negative implications for farming and for rural and urban stability.

This presents a unique challenge to South African land reform. It cannot simply focus on agricultural production, even though the sector needs to be opened up and employment conditions need to be significantly improved.

Land reform has to respond to a broad spectrum of residential needs and it has to do this in a development context which must look beyond agriculture for its productive foundation. Stimulating a non-agricultural rural livelihood base needs to be a national strategic task which goes beyond, but is greater than, the possibilities offered by the land reform project.

RESEARCH REPORTS

Land Reform Research Programme 1995

Land and Agricultural Policy Centre

❐ Western Cape

Administrative and Institutional Structures in the Western Cape Land Reform Process – Fife, Terence. (1994)

Boland Sub-regional Executive Summary – Wentzel, Wilfred. (1994)

Boland Sub-regional Research Report – Wentzel, Wilfred. (1994)

Current Land Struggles and Negotiations in the Western Cape Province – Hofmeyr, Ilne-Mari. (1994)

Employment in Western Cape Agriculture: Implications for Land Reform – Hamman, Johann. (1994)

Engine of Growth: Commercial Agriculture in the Western Cape – Viljoen, J. J.; Eckert, J. B.

Land Reform Research Programme: Provincial Synthesis Report; Western Cape – Wesso, Harold.

Land Reform Research Programme: Provincial Synthesis: Western Cape – Wesso, Harold M.

Land Use and Tenure in the 'Coloured' Rural Reserves, Mission Stations and Other Black Rural Areas of the Western Cape: An Overview – Gilfellan, Calvyn; Primo, Natasha. (1994)

North West District Study: Summary and Detailed Research Reports – Cronwright, Rodney; Marais, Lourens; Squires, Adeline.

Prospects for Land Reform: Western Cape overview.

Prospects for Land Reform in the Western Cape.

Regional Overview of the Western Cape: Implications for Land Reform of Demographic and Socio-Economic Profiles in the Western Cape: Analysis of Data from the Project for Statistics on Living Standards and Development – Mazur, Robert E. (1994)

Women on Farms: Gender Issues in Relation to Land Reform in the Agricultural Sector of the Western Cape Province – Lanz, Sandra Hill; Rossouw, Hester. (1994)

❐ Eastern Cape

Border-Ciskei District Study on Land Reform: Keiskammahoek and Stutterheim District Overviews.

Case Study 1: St Cuthbert's Administrative Area, Tsolo district, Eastern Cape – Mbabana, N; Szucs, I.

Case Study 2: Ngqayi Administrative Area, Qumbu district, Eastern Cape – Mbabana, N; Szucs, I.

Case Study 3: The Umfata Administrative Area, Mount Flecher district, Eastern Cape – Mbabana, N; Szucs, I.

Case Study 4: Umnanga Flats Area, Tsolo district, Eastern Cape – Mbabana, N; Szucs, I.

Case Study 5: Ugie area, Maclear district, Eastern Cape – Mbabana, N; Szucs, I.

Frequency Calculations.

Land Reform Research Programme: Eastern Cape Province; Karoo Sub-Division – James, Bronwyn; Davies, Bill; Gulwa, Busi.

Land Reform Research Programme Eastern Cape Province: Final Synthesis: Draft Report – Van Averbeke, Wim.

Maps and Photographic Documentation of District Study 1: Mfuli, Biyela, Ndundulu.

Overview of the Transkei Sub-Region of the Eastern Cape Province.

Regional Overview of Land Reform: Related Issues in the Eastern Cape Province: Summarising Report – ARDRI; BRC; ISER.

Regional Overview of Land Reform: Related Issues in the Eastern Cape Province – De Wet, Chris; Van Averbeke, Wim.

❒ Northern Cape

An Enumeration and Evaluation of Administrative and Institutional Structures which Serve Rural Land Users in the Northern Cape – Setplan.

Irrigated Crop Production and Land Reform in the Northern Cape – Squires, Stephen.

Land Claims, Negotiations and Land Reform Initiatives in the Northern Cape Province – Dawood, Zohra; Glover, Glenda; Power, Sue; Steyn, Lala.

Land Use Linkages and the Minerals Industry in the Northern Cape and Namaqualand – Solomon, M. H.; Bristow, Dr J. W.

Livestock Production and Land Reform in the Northern Cape – Squires, Stephen.

Northern Cape District Study – Squires, Adeline; Van der Westhuizen, Stephen.

Northern Cape District Study: Summary Report of Five Case Studies – Squires, Adeline; Van der Westhuizen, Stephen.

Provincial Synthesis: Northern Cape Province – Perkins, David.

Regional Overview Report: Northern Cape Province – Perkins, David.

❒ Free State

Agrarian Change, Population Movements and Land Reform in the Free State – Beinart, William; Murray, Colin.

The Agricultural Economy of the Free State.

Agro-Ecological Conditions.

Demographic Profile for the Free State.

Dipatlisiso Ntjhafatsong Ya Kabo Ya Naha Foreistata: Kakaretso ya Raporoto – Heunis, Christo; Tsese, Philemon; Potgieter, Piet.

Free State Rural Restructuring Research Programme: District Study No 2: District Overview – Murray Colin (ed.)

Free State Rural Restructuring Research Programme: District Study No 2; Appendix; Case Studies 1 to 7 – Murray, Colin (ed.).

Free State Workshop Report – Bedford, Laura.

Land Audit [1995]

Land Needs and Related Issues in the 'Northern' Free State: Synthesis of Findings - Botes, L.J.S.; De Wet, M.; Heunis, J. C.

Potential Beneficiaries [1995]

Regional Overview Study of the Free State – Potgieter, Piet.

Regional Overview Study of the Free State: Summary.

Socio-Economic Conditions of the Free State.

Synthesis Report – Bedford, Laura. Land and Agriculture Policy Centre.

Vrystaat Grondhervorming Navorsingprogram: Sinteseveslag – Heunis, Christo; Tsese, Philemon; Potgieter, Piet.

❒ KwaZulu-Natal

2831DA Nkwalini (Map) – Republic of South Africa. Dept. of Surveys and Mapping.

Administrative and Institutional Structures and their Impact on Land Demand - Sapsford, Peter.

Discussion Document on National Environmental Policy.

Dynamics, Conditions and Land Demand in Subsistence Areas within District Study 1 – Sapsford, Peter.

The Forestry Section in KwaZulu-Natal – Saville, Adrian. (1994)

Horticultural Production and Marketing in KwaZulu-Natal – Bedford, Laura.

Institutions Relevant to Land Reform in KwaZulu-Natal – Forsyth, Paul. (1994)

An Investigation into the Dairy Industry in KwaZulu-Natal – Fleming, Colin.

An Investigation into the Red Meat Industry in KwaZulu-Natal – Fleming, Colin.

KwaZulu-Natal Provincial Synthesis Report – Marcus, Tessa.

Land Claims in KwaZulu-Natal – Khosa, Meshack. (1994)

Land Reform Survey Report – Sapsford, Peter.

Land Use and Land Cover of KwaZulu-Natal – Makhanya, Edward. (1994)

Perspectives on Land Demand and Land Reform from the Commercial Agricultural Sector – Vawda, Shahid.

Prospect for Land Reform KwaZulu-Natal Overview – May, Julian; Amin, Nick.

Region E: Economic Development Study; The Agricultural Sector in Region E – Van Zyl, Johan; Von Bach, Helmke Sartorius; Kirsten, Johann. (1993)

Report on Survey Methodology for Land Reform Research Project: District Study 1 – Sapsford, Peter.

Resource Development Directory for Farmworkers - Forsyth, Paul.

A Review of Intrinsic Agricultural Productivity in KwaZulu-Natal: Initial Approaches Results – Schultze, R. E.; Lynch, S. D. (1994)

A Review of Water Demand in KwaZulu-Natal – Quinn, Nevil.

Small Holder Production and Land Demand in KwaZulu-Natal: Case Studies in the Mhlatuze Catchment – Macdonald, Christine; Vaughan, Anne.

Socio-Economic Processes in the Rural Areas of KwaZulu-Natal: Regional Framework for Land Reform Natal-KwaZulu Region – May, Julian. (1994)

The Sugar Industry in KwaZulu Natal - Draper, Peter. (1994)

Synthesis Report District Study One KwaZulu-Natal: Land Demand in the Mhlatuze Catchment: Perspectives from Land Holders and Users – Vaughan, Anne.

Traditional Authorities and Land: The Position in KwaZulu-Natal – McIntosh, Alastair; Sibande, Sipho; Vaughan, Anne; Xaba, Thokozani.

❒ Mpumalanga

Addendum to Eastern Transvaal Land Reform Draft Report: Livestock – Urban-Econ.

Driefontein – TRAC.

Eastern Transvaal: Regional Framework for Land Reform: Agroclimatic Potential and Water Availability – Quinn, Nevil; Horswell, Michael; Lewis, Fonda.

Eastern Transvaal Land Reform: Final Report – Urban-Econ.

Eastern Transvaal Regional Synthesis – Husy, Dave.

Eastern Transvaal Workshop: Presentation of Research Findings.

Evaluation of Nature Based Tourism in the Eastern Transvaal - Scott Wilson Kirkpatrick.

Expanding Smallholder Sugarcane Production in the Eastern Transvaal with Specific Reference to Kangwane – Draper, Peter.

Ezamokuhle – TRAC.

Hlelo: South Eastern Transvaal Case Study – Farmworkers Research and Resource Project.

Horticultural Production and Marketing in the Eastern Transvaal – Bedford, Laura.

Institutions Relevant to Land Reform in the Eastern Transvaal – Chirwa, P D.

Land claims in the Eastern Transvaal : An Overview - Chirwa, P D.

LAPC Workshop Piet Retief – Land and Agriculture Policy Centre.

Prospects for Land Reform in Eastern Transvaal: A Regional Overview – Persad, Ranveer.

South Eastern Transvaal District Study – Toolo, Hilton.

State Centred Approaches to Commercial Small-Holder Development in South Africa: The Case of KaNgwane – McIntosh, Alastair; Vaughan, Anne.

Sulpher Springs: South Eastern Transvaal Case Study – Farmworkers Research and Resource Project.

Zaaihoek: South Eastern Transvaal Case Study – Farmworkers Research and Resource Project.

❒ Northern Province

District Report Far North – Northern Transvaal Land Research Group.

District Report Jane Furse Area: Sekhukhune – Northern Transvaal Land Research Group.

Institutional Support for Rural Restructuring – Eales, Kathy.

Land Research Programme: Northern Transvaal districts - Northern Transvaal LRG.

Northern Transvaal Province Synthesis Report – Forster, Simon F.

Northern Transvaal Regional Overview: Regional Overview Report: A Review of the Findings of the Research Programme – Development Planning and Research.

Northern Transvaal Regional Overview: An Agro-Economic Overview – Van Zyl, Jan; Ferreira, Junior; Butler, Eddie.

Northern Transvaal Regional Overview: A Brief Socio-Demographic Analysis of the Northern Transvaal – Oellermann, Karen.

Northern Transvaal Regional Overview: Land Tenure and Community Legal Issues – Lazarus, Peter; Currie, Lain.

Northern Transvaal Regional Overview: Selected Indicators of Agroclimatic Potential – Quinn, Nevil; Horswell, Michael; Lewis, Fonda.

Overview of the Northern Transvaal and Its Human Resources Potential – Franks, Peter E.

❒ Gauteng

Annexures – Gauteng.

District Case Studies: Gauteng – Gauteng Consortium.

Gauteng Regional Overview Synthesis – Gauteng Consortium.

Synopsis Document: Gauteng Regional Overview: District Case Studies – Gauteng Consortium.

❒ North West

Calculated Fields for Farm and Non-Farm Income and Wealth, and Land Use.

Land Reform Research Programme: North West District Study: Summary and Detailed Research Reports – SETPLAN.

North-West District Study: Synthesis Report and Case Studies – SETPLAN.

North West Provincial Study on Land Reform: Dynthesis Focument – Burns, Justine (ed.)

A Regional Overview Study of the North West.

A Regional Overview Study of the North West Province – Kalakaroo.

Administrative and Institutional Structures.

REFERENCES

Ainslee A, Fox R and Fabricius C (1995) 'Towards Policies for Feasible and Sustainable Natural Resource Use: The Mid-Fish River Zonal Study, Eastern Cape'. LAPC NRM Case Studies: Summary Reports of Zonal Studies, Working Paper 15, 1995. LAPC Johannesburg.

Attwood H, Christensen AK and Gothold ML (1995) 'LAPC Land Reform Research: National Report, Vol 1'. LAPC, Johannesburg.

Bank L and Southall R (undated) 'Traditional Leaders Under the Constitution in South Africa's New Democracy'. Submission to the Constitutional Assembly, Cape Town.

Beinart W (1994) 'Farmers Strategies and Land Reform in the OFS', *in Review of African Political Economy* No 61.

Bernstein A (ed) (1994) 'Urban Land Invasion: The International Experience'. Urban Foundation Development Strategy and Policy Unit, Johannesburg.

Bromley DW (1995) 'Natural Resource Issues in Environmental Policy in South Africa'. LAPC, July 1995. Johannesburg.

Brown J et al (eds) (1991) *History from South Africa: Alternative Visions and Practices.* Temple University Press, Philadelphia

Centre for Applied Legal Studies (undated) 'Submission to Theme Group 4 on the Property Clause'. Land Rights Project, Centre for Applied Legal Studies, Johannesburg. Mimeo. Submission to the Constitutional Assembly, Cape Town.

Claasens A (1995) 'Land Rights and the Property Clause'. Constitutional Assembly Theme Committee 6 Workshop on 'Land Rights and the Constitution', August 1-2. Cape Town.

Commission of Inquiry into the Provision of Rural Financial Services (1995) 'Commission of Inquiry into the Provision of Rural Financial Services: Interim Report No 1'. Unpublished report.

Commission on Provincial Government (1995) 'Preliminary Recommendations on Traditional Authorities', Recommendations Document 8. May 29, 1995, Constitutional Assembly. Cape Town.

Coldham S (1978) 'The Effect of Registration of Title upon Customary Land Rights in Kenya', in Journal *of African Law* No 91.

Constitutional Assembly (1995) *Working Draft of the New Constitution*, November 22, 1995. Government Printers, Cape Town.

Constitutional Assembly (1995) 'Land Rights and the Constitution', workshop report by Technical Advisers to Theme Committee 6.3. August 18, 1995, Constitutional Assembly. Cape Town.

Cramb RA and Wills IR (1990) 'Agrarian Reform, Peasant and Rural Production and the Organisation of Production in the Transition to Socialism', in Fagan R, Deere CD and Coraggio JL (eds) *Transition and Development: Problems of Third World Socialism*. Monthly Review Press.

Cross C (1987) 'The Land Reform Question in KwaZulu: Is Land Reform Necessary?', in *Development Southern Africa* Vol 4 No 3, August 1987.

Cross C (1992) 'Property Rights in Relation to South African Land Reform', in *South African Journal on Human Rights*, 305 at 313.

Cross C (1995) 'Losing the Land: Securing Tenure in Tribal Areas', in *Indicator SA* Vol 12 No 2, Autumn 1995. University of Natal, Durban.

Davis D, Chaskalson M and de Waal J (1994) 'Democracy and Constitutionalism: The Role of Constitutional Interpretation', in Van Wyk S, Dugard J, De Villiers B and Davis D *Rights and Constitutionalism: The New South African Legal Order*. Juta, Cape Town.

Erasmus J (1994) *South Africa's Nine Provinces: A Human Development Profile. 1994.* Development Bank of Southern Africa, Johannesburg.

Development Planning and Research (1995) 'Mpumalanga Pilot Land Reform Programme: Stakeholder Analysis'. Unpublished report commissioned by the Department of Land and Housing, Mpumalanga Government, September 1985. Mpumalanga.

De Wet C (1994) 'Resettlement and Land Reform in South Africa', *in Review of African Political Economy* No 61.

Evans P (1995) *Embedded Autonomy: States and Industrial Transformation*. Princeton University Press, Princeton.

Farrington J, Bebbington A, Wellard K and Lewis D (1993) *Reluctant Partners? Non Governmental Organisations, the State and Sustainable Agricultural Development*.

Gluckman M (1967) *Politics, Law and Ritual in Tribal Society*. Basil Blackwell, Oxford.

Hosten Edwards Natal and Bosman (1977) *Introduction to South African Law and Theory*. Butterworth.

Horn (1994) 'Women and the Labour Market: Challenges Posed for Job Creation Policy', in *Transformation* No 25. University of Natal, Durban.

Kerr AJ (1994) 'Customary Law, Fundamental Rights and the Constitution', in *The South African Law Journal* Vol 11 Part IV, November 1994.

Kingwill R (1992) 'Land is More than a Plot Fenced In. Land Reform: Perspectives of a Just Land Distribution'. Unpublished paper presented at the conference, 'Development Perspectives in Southern Africa — Perspectives for Solidarity Work'. Germany.

Letsoalo EM (1987) *Land Reform in South Africa:A Black Perspective*. Skotaville.

Letsoalo EM (no date) 'The Land Issue in South Africa: Making Informed Decisions'. Unpublished paper.

Levin R (1993) 'The Agrarian Question and Politics in the 'New' South Africa', in Review of African Political Economy No 57.

Levin R (1994) 'Participatory Research and Democratic Agrarian Transformation: The Case of the Eastern Transvaal Central Lowveld', in Transformation No 25. University of Natal, Durban.

Levin R and Weiner D (eds) (1994) Community Perspectives on Land and Agrarian Reform in South Africa.

Marcus T (1994) 'Land Reform in Rural Restructuring Programmes: Comparative Policy Approaches and Experiences from the Developing World', in Development Southern Africa V11 No 4, 1994.

Marks S and Atmore A (eds) (1980) Economy and Society in Pre-Industrial South Africa. Longman.

May J (1994) 'How Green is Your Garden?', in Indicator SA Vol 11 No 3, Winter 1994. University of Natal, Durban.

Murray C and Williams G (1994) 'Land and Freedom in South Africa', in Review of African Political Economy No 61.

McIntosh A and Vaughan A (1994) 'Towards a System of Rural local Government for the Northern Transvaal'. Working Paper 34. Development Bank of Southern Africa, Johannesburg.

McKenzie C (1994) 'Degradation of Arable Land Resources: Policy Options and Considerations Within the Context of Rural Restructuring in South Africa'. LAPC Policy Paper 11, December 1994. Johannesburg.

Nyamapfene K (1995) 'Lessons from the Land Reform Programmes of Other Countries: A contribution to the Proposed Land Reform Framework for South Africa. LAPC. Johannesburg.

Saldru (1994) 'South Africans Rich and Poor: Baseline Household Statistics Project', for Statistics on Living Standards and Development School of Economics. University of Cape Town, Cape Town.

Singini R and Van Rooyen J (eds) (1995) 'Serving Small Scale Farmers: An Evaluation of the DBSA's Farmer Support Programmes'. Development Bank of Southern Africa, Johannesburg.

Surplus People Project (1995) 'Land Claims in Namaqualand'. Surplus People Project.

Thompson L (1994) 'Women and Agricultural Development in Southern Africa: Lessons for the New South African Government'. Centre for Rural Legal Studies, Discussion paper. Johannesburg.

Van der Walt A J (1994) 'Property Rights, Land Rights and Environmental Rights', in Van Wyk S, Dugard J, De Villiers B and Davis D Rights and Constitutionalism: The New South African Legal Order. Juta, Cape Town.

Van der Walt A J (1995) 'Land Reform in South Africa Since 1990 – An Overview', in SA Public Law Vol 10 No 1, 1995. University of South Africa, Pretoria.

Van Wyk D (1994) 'Introduction to the South African Constitution', in Van Wyk S, Dugard J, De Villiers B and Davis D Rights and Constitutionalism: The New South African Legal Order. Juta and Co.

Walker C (1994) 'Women, "Tradition" and Reconstruction', in Review of African Political Economy No 61.

Williams G (1993) 'Rural Restructuring. The World Bank's Options', in Indicator SA Vol 11 No 1, Summer 1993. University of Natal, Durban.